The Social Life of Small Urban Spaces

To Our Readers

For more than 25 years, Project for Public Spaces has been using observations, surveys, interviews and workshops to study and transform public spaces around the world into community places. Every week we give presentations about why some public spaces work and why others don't, using the techniques, ideas, and memorable phrases from William H. "Holly" Whyte's The Social Life of Small Urban Spaces.

In our effort to create and sustain public spaces that build communities, Project for Public Spaces runs programs in markets, transportation, parks and civic squares, and public buildings. Our Public Market Collaborative uses open-air and historic downtown markets to transform streets, plazas, and parking lots into bustling "people places," alive with vitality and commerce. Our programs in transportation are helping to reduce sprawl and create more livable communities by encouraging the use of transit and traffic calming. And we manage the Urban Parks Institute, which promotes parks as community places. We also conduct training programs for all kinds of professionals, from traffic engineers to architects, as well as for communities and government officials, to help them understand what we learned from Holly—that it's places that matter, not projects, and that in order to function as true gathering places, public spaces must be designed with people and uses in mind. All these concepts are tied together in How to Turn a Place Around, a handbook for creating the kinds of thriving, social places that The Social Life of Small Urban Spaces first identified.

Holly Whyte was both our mentor and our friend. Perhaps his most important gift was the ability to show us how to discover for ourselves why some public spaces work and others don't. With the publication of The Social Life of Small Urban Spaces and its companion film in 1980, the world could see that through the basic tools of observation and interviews, we can learn an immense amount about how to make our cities more livable. In doing so, Holly Whyte laid the groundwork for a major movement to change the way public spaces are built and planned. It is our pleasure to offer this important book back to the world it is helping to transform.

Fred Kent, *President*
Steve Davies and Kathy Madden, *Vice Presidents*

PROJECT FOR PUBLIC SPACES
153 Waverly Place, 4th Floor
New York, NY 10014
(212) 620-5660
www.pps.org

The Social Life of Small Urban Spaces

by William H. Whyte

Project for Public Spaces
New York, NY

Contents

Foreword

Toward the end of *The Last Landscape,* a book that begins in the countryside of Pennsylvania, William H. Whyte writes of driving along the highway, approaching U.S. cities, searching without success for their boundaries among monotonous roadside clutter. For the last ten years, he has spent much of his time in the thick of the cities, particularly in New York. He has been looking at city space, talking with people, making notes, taking photographs and films, measuring the heights of benches and ledges, writing articles, helping to draft zoning ordinances, speaking in church basements and tall buildings, discovering the public places that people use and don't use, and why. And, as you will discover, he has often been surprised.

I, too, was surprised several years ago, when Holly Whyte spoke to a gathering at New York's Municipal Art Society. Most people at that time associated New York with dirt, decay, crime, and fiscal crisis. "I'm going to show you some film of people walking the streets of Manhattan," he said, "and I want you to look for what these people have in common." Feet. Shoes. Legs. Pants. Shirts. Blouses. Skirts. Arms. Purses. Briefcases. Umbrellas. Heads. Hats. Hard hats. Faces. Smiles. Smiles? Why should people on New York streets be smiling?

They were happy—in the midst of urban crisis, on the streets of a city that many thought was going under. Of course, there were other people on the streets without smiles, maybe even scowling. But when we think of cities and the people in them, we have been too much inclined to forget the smile altogether. There are happy people in cities. There are healthy places that people like in cities, places that contribute to happiness, places that can bring out that smile.

Those places include some of the small urban spaces that this book is about. Successful miniparks, like Paley or Greenacre in New York, Farragut Square or Dupont Circle in Washington. Or plazas, like the one at the First National Bank in Chicago. And ledges, along the street and around fountains, where people sit and pass the time of day.

In the following pages, Whyte describes how small urban spaces work and don't work. That is, what gives them life or kills them. What draws people. What keeps them out. Spaces designed to keep out undesirables—pushers, bums, hippies—for example, generally tend to keep out other people, too. In contrast, spaces that attract people tend to be relatively free of problems. The sun is important. So are trees and water and food and, most of all, seats. These are the things you will learn from this book, things that should not be surprising, but often are. (You will also learn about how to use cameras as a research tool!)

Why should conservationists care what the people in New York City streets are doing? Thirty, twenty, perhaps even ten years ago, we might have parted ways with Whyte somewhere along that highway into the city. The challenge for conservationists, then as now, was to preserve nature, wildlife and wilderness, open space, agricultural and undeveloped land. But when we beheld the city, we beheld the behemoth. Its advance had to be stopped. But it couldn't be.

And it can't be now. Not without creative development to provide housing and meet the other demands of a growing population. Not unless we match our efforts to conserve the countryside with efforts to conserve the city. Quite simply, if people find cities uninhabitable, they will want to move out of them. So our challenge is to conserve both country *and* city. That is why in 1975, with the cosponsorship of the first major national conference on neighborhood conservation, The Conservation Foundation began its work in urban conservation. That is why we are interested in *The Social Life of Small Urban Spaces.*

Collectively, a city's abundant small spaces have a major impact on the quality of life. If those spaces are unattractive, people will likely retreat from the city street, perhaps from the city itself—to the suburbs and country if they can manage it, to fortified shelters in cities if they cannot. But if we learn to take advantage of our small urban spaces, if we design new ones well, and fix up the old ones, we will keep the streets alive. We may even encourage more people to use them, and to smile about it.

William K. Reilly, President
The Conservation Foundation

Preface

This is a pre-book. When I started the Street Life Project in 1971, it was with the expectation that our research would last about two years and that I would then pull the findings into a book. At the very latest, I told Doubleday & Co., 1974. As is often the way with projects, however, the research grew and grew. Our initial studies of playgrounds led to a project on teen-age territories; our studies of New York's most crowded street led to a request to do a similar study in Tokyo; a study of indoor spaces led to comparison studies of suburban shopping malls. So it went. A year ago, I swore off more research and started writing.

Most of our research has been fundamental—that is, I can't now think of any especial applicability for it. What has fascinated us most is the behavior of ordinary people on city streets—their rituals in street encounters, for example, the regularity of chance meetings, the tendency to reciprocal gestures in street conferences, the rhythms of the three-phase good-bye. By the time the full book is finished, I am sure I will have figured out much more significance to all this. But not quite yet.

There is one part of our work, however, which does have immediate applicability: our study of spaces that work, don't work, and the reasons why. Rather than wait for completion of the book, I thought it would be helpful to get out our findings and recommendations, and thus this manual. I am indebted to The Conservation

Foundation and its president, William K. Reilly, for publishing it, and to Robert McCoy for his editorial help.

As a companion to the manual I have completed a 55-minute film—with the same title and the same general structure. It is being distributed under the auspices of the Municipal Art Society of New York. I want to express my thanks to Executive Director Margot Wellington, and to President Doris Freedman, one of the reasons many New York spaces so delight the eye and spirit.

The main work of the Street Life Project was done by a small band of young observers, and I want to thank them for their curiosity, their diligence, and their tendency to dispute my hypotheses. The principal researchers the first years were Marilyn Russell and Nancy Linday. They were joined by Fred Kent, Ellen Ascher, Margaret Bemiss, Ann Herendeen, and Elizabeth Dietel. Working with us on special studies were: Beverly Peyser, Ellen Iseman, Cecilia Rubin, and Ann R. Roberts.

For their help on many things, I want to thank Raquel Ramati and Michael Parley of the Urban Design Group of the New York City Planning Department, and Kenneth Halpern and Loren Otis of the Mayor's Office of Midtown Planning and Development.

I have many organizations to thank. The basic research was a project of the National Recreation and Park Association and was supported by grants from the Vincent Astor Foundation, the National Geographic Society, the National Endowment for the Arts, the Rockefeller Brothers Fund, the Rockefeller Family Fund, and the Fund for the City of New York. A grant for the preparation of this publication was provided by the Graham Foundation for Advanced Studies in the Fine Arts. The film project was made possible by public funds from the New York State Council on the Arts, and by grants from the American Conservation Association, the J. M. Kaplan Fund, Joseph E. Seagram & Sons, Inc., the New York Telephone Company, and the Arthur Ross Foundation.

I thank these good people for their support and their interest, and their patience. Finally, I want to thank Laurance S. Rockefeller—for his support of our work, and for helping bring about some of the most felicitous of small urban spaces.

William H. Whyte
New York, New York
January 1980

Introduction

This book is about city spaces, why some work for people, and some do not, and what the practical lessons may be. It is a by-product of first-hand observation.

In 1970, I formed a small research group, The Street Life Project, and began looking at city spaces. At that time, direct observation had long been used for the study of people in far-off lands. It had not been used to any great extent in the U.S. city. There was much concern over urban crowding, but most of the research on the issue was done somewhere other than where it supposedly occurred. The most notable studies were of crowded animals, or of students and members of institutions responding to experimental situations— often valuable research, to be sure, but somewhat vicarious.

The Street Life Project began its study by looking at New York City parks and playgrounds and such informal recreation areas as city blocks. One of the first things that struck us was the *lack* of crowding in many of these areas. A few were jammed, but more were nearer empty than full, often in neighborhoods that ranked very high in density of people. Sheer space, obviously, was not of itself attracting children. Many streets were.

It is often assumed that children play in the street because they lack playground space. But many children play in the streets because they like to. One of the best play areas we came across was a block on 101st Street in East Harlem. It had its

101st Street, East Harlem.

Seagram's

problems, but it worked. The street itself was the play area. Adjoining stoops and fire escapes provided prime viewing across the street and were highly functional for mothers and older people. There were other factors at work, too, and, had we been more prescient, we could have saved ourselves a lot of time spent later looking at plazas. Though we did not know it then, this block had within it all the basic elements of a successful urban place.

As our studies took us nearer the center of New York, the imbalance in space use was even more apparent. Most of the

crowding could be traced to a series of choke points—subway stations, in particular. In total, these spaces are only a fraction of downtown, but the number of people using them is so high, the experience so abysmal, that it colors our perception of the city around, out of all proportion to the space involved. The fact that there may be lots of empty space somewhere else little mitigates the discomfort. And there is a strong carry-over effect.

This affects researchers, too. We see what we expect to see, and have been so conditioned to see crowded spaces in center city that it is often difficult to see empty ones. But when we looked, there they were.

The amount of space, furthermore, was increasing. Since 1961, New York City has been giving incentive bonuses to builders who provided plazas. For each square foot of plaza, builders could add 10 square feet of commercial floor space over and above the amount normally permitted by zoning. So they did—without exception. Every new office building provided a plaza or comparable space: in total, by 1972, some 20 acres of the world's most expensive open space.

We discovered that some plazas, especially at lunchtime, attracted a lot of people. One, the plaza of the Seagram Building, was the place that helped give the city the idea for the plaza bonus. Built in 1958, this austerely elegant area had not been planned as a people's plaza, but that is what it became. On a good day, there would be a hundred and fifty people sitting, sunbathing, picnicking, and shmoozing—idly gossiping, talking "nothing talk." People also liked 77 Water Street, known as "swingers' plaza" because of the young crowd that populated it.

But on most plazas, we didn't see many people. The plazas weren't used for much except walking across. In the middle of the lunch hour on a beautiful, sunny day the number of people sitting on plazas averaged four per 1,000 square feet of space—an extraordinarily low figure for so dense a center. The tightest-knit CBD (central business district) anywhere contained a surprising amount of open space that was relatively empty and unused.

If places like Seagram's and 77 Water Street could work so well, why not the others? The city was being had. For the millions of dollars of extra space it was handing out to builders, it had every right to demand much better plazas in return.

I put the question to the chairman of the City Planning Commission, Donald Elliott. As a matter of fact, I entrapped him into spending a weekend looking at time-lapse films of plaza use and nonuse. He felt that tougher zoning was in order. If we could find out why the good plazas worked and the bad ones didn't, and come up with hard guidelines, we could have the basis of a new code. Since we could expect the proposals to be strongly contested, it would be important to document the case to a fare-thee-well.

We set to work. We began studying a cross-section of spaces—in all, 16 plazas, 3 small parks, and a number of odds and ends. I will pass over the false starts, the dead ends, and the floundering arounds, save to note that there were a lot and that the research was nowhere as tidy and sequential as it can seem in the telling. Let me also note that the findings should have been staggeringly obvious to us had we thought of them in the first place. But we didn't. Opposite propositions were often what seemed obvious. We arrived at our eventual findings by a succession of busted hypotheses.

The research continued for some three years. I like to cite the figure because it sounds impressive. But it is calendar time. For all practical purposes, at the end of six months we had completed our basic

research and arrived at our recommendations. The City, alas, had other concerns on its mind, and we found that communicating the findings was to take more time than arriving at them. We logged many hours in church basements and meeting rooms giving film and slide presentations to community groups, architects, planners, businessmen, developers, and real-estate people. We continued our research; we had to keep our findings up-to-date, for

now we were disciplined by adversaries. But at length the City Planning Commission incorporated our recommendations in a proposed new open-space zoning code, and in May 1975 it was adopted by the city's Board of Estimate. As a consequence, there has been a salutary improvement in the design of new spaces and the rejuvenation of old ones. (Since the zoning may have useful guidelines for other cities, an abridged text is provided as appendix B.)

But zoning is certainly not the ideal way to achieve the better design of spaces. It ought to be done for its own sake. For economics alone, it makes sense. An enormous expenditure of design expertise, and of travertine and steel, went into the creation of the many really bum office-building plazas around the country. To what end? As this manual will detail, it is far easier, simpler to create spaces that work for people than those that do not—and a tremendous difference it can make to the life of a city.

The Life of Plazas

1

We started by studying how people use plazas. We mounted time-lapse cameras overlooking the plazas and recorded daily patterns. We talked to people to find where they came from, where they worked, how frequently they used the place and what they thought of it. But, mostly, we watched people to see what they did.

Most of the people who use plazas, we found, are young office workers from nearby buildings. There may be relatively few patrons from the plaza's own building; as some secretaries confide, they'd just as soon put a little distance between themselves and the boss. But commuter distances are usually short; for most plazas, the effective market radius is about three blocks. Small parks, like Paley and Greenacre in New York, tend to have more assorted patrons throughout the day—upper-income older people, people coming from a distance. But office workers still predominate, the bulk from nearby.

This uncomplicated demography underscores an elemental point about good urban spaces: supply creates demand. A good new space builds a new constituency. It stimulates people into new habits—al fresco lunches—and provides new paths to and from work, new places to pause. It does all this very quickly. In Chicago's Loop, there were no such amenities not so long ago. Now, the plaza of the First National Bank has thoroughly changed the midday way of life for thousands of people. A success like this in no way surfeits demand for spaces; it indicates how great the unrealized potential is.

The best-used plazas are sociable places, with a higher proportion of couples than you find in less-used places, more people in groups, more people meeting people, or exchanging goodbyes. At five of the most-used plazas in New York, the proportion of people in groups runs about 45 percent; in five of the least used, 32 percent. A high proportion of people in groups is an index of selectivity. When people go to a place in twos or threes or rendezvous there, it is most often because they have decided to. Nor are these sociable places less congenial to the individual. In absolute numbers, they attract more individuals than do less-used spaces. If you

Above: Paley Park.
Below: A useful sculpture exhibit at Seagram's plaza.

are alone, a lively place can be the best place to be.

The most-used places also tend to have a higher than average proportion of women. The male-female ratio of a plaza basically reflects the composition of the work force, which varies from area to area—in midtown New York it runs about 60 percent male, 40 percent female. Women are more discriminating than men as to where they will sit, more sensitive to annoyances, and women spend more time casting the various possibilities. If a plaza has a markedly lower than average proportion of women, something is wrong. Where there is a higher than average proportion of women, the plaza is probably a good one and has been chosen as such.

The rhythms of plaza life are much alike from place to place. In the morning hours, patronage will be sporadic. A hot-dog vendor setting up his cart at the corner, elderly pedestrians pausing for a rest, a delivery messenger or two, a shoeshine man, some tourists, perhaps an odd type, like a scavenger woman with shopping bags. If there is any construction work in the vicinity, hard hats will appear shortly after 11:00 A.M. with beer cans and sandwiches. Things will start to liven up. Around noon, the main clientele begins to arrive. Soon, activity will be near peak and will stay there until a little before 2:00 P.M. Some 80 percent of the total hours of use will be concentrated in these two hours. In mid and late afternoon, use is again sporadic. If there's a special event, such as a jazz concert, the flow going home will be tapped, with people staying as late as 6:00 or 6:30 P.M. Ordinarily, however, plazas go dead by 6:00 and stay that way until the next morning.

During peak hours the number of people on a plaza will vary considerably according to seasons and weather. The way people distribute themselves over the space, however, will be fairly consistent, with some sectors getting heavy use day in and day out, others much less. In our sightings we find it easy to map every person, but the patterns are regular enough that you could count the number in only one sector, then multiply by a given factor, and come within a percent or so of the total number of people at the plaza.

Off-peak use often gives the best clues to people's preferences. When a place is jammed, a person sits where he can. This may or may not be where he most wants to. After the main crowd has left, the choices can be significant. Some parts of the plaza become quite empty; others continue to be used. At Seagram's, a rear ledge under the trees is moderately, but steadily, occupied when other ledges are empty; it seems the most uncrowded of places, but on a cumulative basis it is the best-used part of Seagram's.

Men show a tendency to take the front-row seats, and, if there is a kind of gate, men will be the guardians of it. Women tend to favor places slightly secluded. If there are double-sided benches parallel to a street, the inner side will usually have a high proportion of women; the outer, of men.

Of the men up front, the most conspicuous are girl watchers. They work at it, and so demonstratively as to suggest that their chief interest may not really be the girls so much as the show of watching them. Generally, the watchers line up quite close together, in groups of three to five. If they are construction workers, they will be very demonstrative, much given to whistling, laughing, direct salutations. This is also true of most girl watchers in New York's financial area. In midtown, they are more inhibited, playing it coolly, with a good bit of sniggering and smirking, as if the girls were not measuring up. It is all machismo, however, whether uptown or downtown. Not once have we ever seen a girl watcher pick up a girl, or attempt to.

Few others will either. Plazas are not

ideal places for striking up acquaintances, and even on the most sociable of them, there is not much mingling. When strangers are in proximity, the nearest thing to an exchange is what Erving Goffman has called civil inattention. If there are, say, two smashing blondes on a ledge, the men nearby will usually put on an elaborate show of disregard. Watch closely, however, and you will see them give themselves away with covert glances, involuntary primping of the hair, tugs at the earlobe.

Lovers are to be found on plazas. But not where you would expect them. When we first started interviewing, people told us we'd find lovers in the rear places (pot smokers, too). But they weren't usually there. They would be out front. The most fervent embracing we've recorded on film has usually taken place in the most visible of locations, with the couple oblivious of the crowd.

Certain locations become rendezvous points for coteries of various kinds. For a while, the south wall of Chase plaza was a gathering point for camera bugs, the kind who like to buy new lenses and talk about them. Patterns of this sort may last no more than a season—or persist for years.

Some time ago, one particular spot became a gathering place for raffish younger people; since then, there have been many changeovers in personnel, but it is still a gathering place for raffish younger people.

Self-Congestion

What attracts people most, it would appear, is other people. If I belabor the point, it is because many urban spaces are being designed as though the opposite were true, and that what people liked best were the places they stay away from. People often do talk along such lines; this is why their responses to questionnaires can be so misleading. How many people would say they like to sit in the middle of a crowd? Instead, they speak of getting away from it all, and use terms like "escape," "oasis," "retreat." What people *do*, however, reveals a different priority.

This was first brought home to us in a study of street conversations. When people stop to have a conversation, we wondered, how far away do they move from the main pedestrian flow? We were especially interested in finding out how much of the normally unused buffer space next

to buildings would be used. So we set up time-lapse cameras overlooking several key street corners and began plotting the location of all conversations lasting a minute or longer.

People didn't move out of the main pedestrian flow. They stayed in it or moved into it, and the great bulk of the conversations were smack in the center of the flow—the 100 percent location, to use the real-estate term. The same gravitation characterized "traveling conversations"—the kind in which two men move about, alternating the roles of straight man and principal talker. There is a lot of apparent motion. But if you plot the orbits, you will find they are usually centered around the 100 percent spot.

Just why people behave like this, we have never been able to determine. It is understandable that conversations should originate within the main flow. Conversations are incident to pedestrian journeys; where there are the most people, the likelihood of a meeting or a leave-taking is highest. What is less explainable is people's inclination to remain in the main flow, blocking traffic, being jostled by it.

This does not seem to be a matter of inertia but of choice—instinctive, perhaps, but by no means illogical. In the center of the crowd you have the maximum choice—to break off, to continue—much as you have in the center of a cocktail party, itself a moving conversation growing ever denser and denser.

People also sit in the mainstream. At the Seagram plaza, the main pedestrian paths are on diagonals from the building entrance to the corners of the steps. These are natural junction and transfer points and there is usually a lot of activity at them. They are also a favored place for sitting and picnicking. Sometimes there will be so many people that pedestrians have to step carefully to negotiate the steps. The pedestrians rarely complain. While some will detour around the blockage, most will thread their way through it.

Standing patterns are similar. When people stop to talk on a plaza, they usually do so in the middle of the traffic stream. They also show an inclination to station themselves near objects, such as a flagpole or a statue. They like well-defined places, such as steps, or the border of a pool.

21

What they rarely choose is the middle of a large space.

There are a number of explanations. The preference for pillars might be ascribed to some primeval instinct: you have a full view of all comers but your rear is covered. But this doesn't explain the inclination men have for lining up at the curb. Typically, they face inwards, toward the sidewalk, with their backs exposed to the dangers of the street.

Foot movements are consistent, too. They seem to be a sort of silent language. Often, in a shmoozing group no one will be saying anything. Men stand bound in amiable silence, surveying the passing scene. Then, slowly, rhythmically, one of the men rocks up and down: first on the ball of the foot, then back on the heel. He stops. Another man starts the same movement. Sometimes there are reciprocal gestures. One man makes a half turn to the right. Then, after a rhythmic interval, another responds with a half turn to the left. Some kind of communication seems to be taking place here, but I've never broken the code.

Whatever they may mean, people's movements are one of the great spectacles of a plaza. You do not see this in architectural photographs, which typically are empty of life and are taken from a perspective few people share. It is a quite misleading one. At eye level the scene comes alive with movement and color— people walking quickly, walking slowly, skipping up steps, weaving in and out on crossing patterns, accelerating and retarding to match the moves of the others. There is a beauty that is beguiling to watch, and one senses that the players are quite aware of it themselves. You see this, too, in the way they arrange themselves on steps and ledges. They often do so with a grace that they, too, must sense. With its brown-gray monochrome, Seagram's is the best of settings—especially in the rain, when an umbrella or two spots

color in the right places, like Corot's red dots.

How peculiar are such patterns to New York? Our working assumption was that behavior in other cities would probably differ little, and subsequent comparisons have proved our assumption correct. The important variable is city size. As I will discuss in more detail, in smaller cities, densities tend to be lower, pedestrians move at a slower pace, and there is less of the social activity characteristic of high-traffic areas. In most other respects, pedestrian patterns are similar.

Observers in other countries have also noted the tendency to self-congestion. In his study of pedestrians in Copenhagen, architect Jan Gehl mapped bunching patterns almost identical to those observable here. Matthew Ciolek studied an Australian shopping center, with similar results.

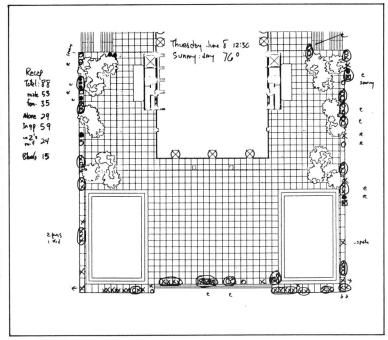

Left: The new parklet in front of the Boston Five-Cent Savings Bank has become one of Old Boston's most congenial gathering places.

This is a typical sighting map. We found that one could map the location of every sitter, whether male (X), female (O), alone, or with others (XO), in about five minutes, little more time than a simple head count would take.

"Contrary to 'common sense' expectations," Ciolek notes, "the great majority of people were found to select their sites for social interaction right on or very close to the traffic lines intersecting the plaza. Relatively few people formed their gatherings away from the spaces used for navigation."

The strongest similarities are found among the world's largest cities. People in them tend to behave more like their counterparts in other world cities than like fellow nationals in smaller cities. Big-city people walk faster, for one thing, and they self-congest. After we had completed our New York study, we made a brief comparison study of Tokyo and found the proclivity to stop and talk in the middle of department-store doorways, busy corners, and the like, is just as strong in that city as in New York. For all the cultural differences, sitting patterns in parks and plazas are much the same, too. Similarly, shmoozing patterns in Milan's Galleria are remarkably like those in New York's garment center. Modest conclusion: given the basic elements of a center city—such as high pedestrian volumes, and concentration and mixture of activities—people in one place tend to act much like people in another.

Sitting Space

2

In their use of plazas, New Yorkers were very consistent. Day in, day out, many of them would sit at certain plazas, few at others. On the face of it, there should not have been this variance. Most of the plazas we were studying were fairly comparable. With few exceptions, they were on major avenues and usually occupied a block front. They were close to bus stops and subway stations and had strong pedestrian flows on the sidewalks beside them. Yet when we rated plazas according to the number of people sitting on them at peak time, there was a very wide range—from 160 people at 77 Water Street to 17 at 280 Park Avenue (see chart 1).

How come? The first factor we studied was the sun. We thought it might well be the critical one, and our initial time-lapse studies seemed to bear this out. Subsequent studies did not. As I will note later, they showed that the sun was important, but did not explain the difference in the popularity of plazas.

Nor did aesthetics. We never thought ourselves capable of measuring such factors, but did expect our research to show the most successful plazas would tend to be the most pleasing visually. Seagram's seemed very much a case in point. Here again, the evidence proved conflicting. Not only was clean, elegant Seagram's successful; so was the fun plaza at 77 Water Street, which some architects look on as kitsch. We also noticed that the elegance and purity of a building's design seems to

Above: The ledge at St. Peter's Church, part of the Citicorp complex, has become one of the most-used sitting places on Lexington Avenue.

Left: Another popular place to tarry is a simple round bench at Rockefeller Center, just across the street from St. Patrick's Cathedral.

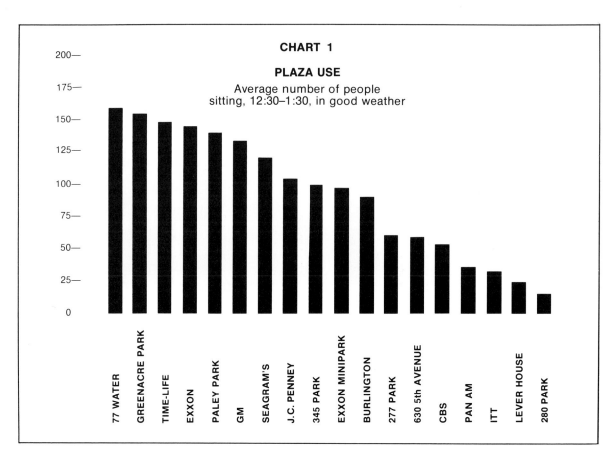

CHART 1

PLAZA USE

Average number of people
sitting, 12:30–1:30, in good weather

200—
175—
150—
125—
100—
75—
50—
25—
0

77 WATER
GREENACRE PARK
TIME-LIFE
EXXON
PALEY PARK
GM
SEAGRAM'S
J.C. PENNEY
345 PARK
EXXON MINIPARK
BURLINGTON
277 PARK
630 5th AVENUE
CBS
PAN AM
ITT
LEVER HOUSE
280 PARK

have little relationship to the use of the spaces around it.

The designer sees the whole building—the clean verticals, the horizontals, the way Mies turned his corners, and so on. The person sitting on the plaza may be quite unaware of such matters. He is more apt to be looking in the other direction: not up at other buildings, but at what is going on at eye level. To say this is not to slight the designer's eye or his handling of space. The area around Seagram's is a great urban place and its relationship to McKim, Mead & White's Racquet Club across the street is integral to it. My personal feeling is that a sense of enclosure contributes to the enjoyment of using the Seagram plaza. But I certainly can't prove this with figures.

Another factor we considered was

shape. Urban designers believed this was extremely important and hoped our findings might support tight criteria for proportions and placement. They were particularly anxious to rule out "strip plazas"—long narrow spaces that were little more than enlarged sidewalks, and empty more often than not. Designers felt a developer shouldn't get bonuses for these strips, and to this end they wanted to rule out spaces the length of which was more than three times the width.

Our data did not support such criteria. We found that most strip plazas were, indeed, empty of people most of the time. But was the shape the cause? Some square plazas were empty, too, and several of the most heavily used places were, in fact, long narrow strips. One of the five most popular sitting places in New York is es-

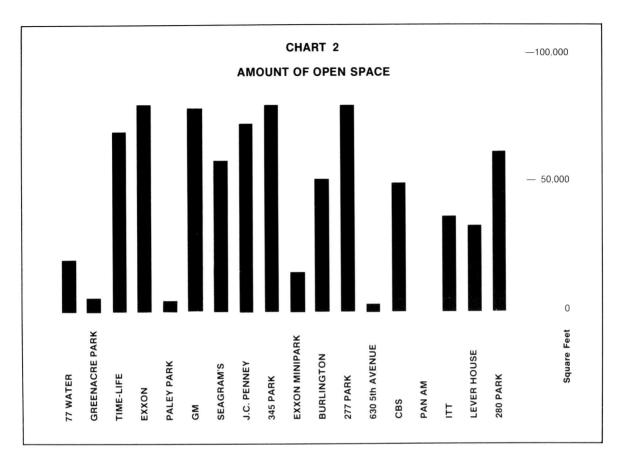

CHART 2

AMOUNT OF OPEN SPACE

—100,000

— 50,000

0

Square Feet

77 WATER · GREENACRE PARK · TIME-LIFE · EXXON · PALEY PARK · GM · SEAGRAM'S · J.C. PENNEY · 345 PARK · EXXON MINIPARK · BURLINGTON · 277 PARK · 630 5th AVENUE · CBS · PAN AM · ITT · LEVER HOUSE · 280 PARK

sentially an indentation in a building—and long and narrow. Our research did not prove shape unimportant or designers' instincts misguided; as with the sun, however, it did prove that other factors were more critical.

If not shape, could the *amount* of space be the key factor? Some conservationists were sure this would be it. In their view, people seek open spaces as a relief from the overcrowding they are normally subjected to, and it would follow that places affording the greatest feeling of light and space would draw the most. If we ranked plazas by the amount of space, there surely would be a positive correlation between the size of the plazas and the number of persons using them.

Once again, we found no clear relationship. As can be seen in chart 2, several of

the smaller spaces had lots of people, several of the larger had lots of people, and several of the larger had very few people. Sheer space, it appears, does not draw people. In some circumstances, it can have the opposite effect.

What about the amount of *sittable* space? Here we begin to get close. As chart 3 shows, the most popular plazas tend to have considerably more sitting space than the less well-used ones. The relationship is rough. For one reason, the amount of sitting space does not include any qualitative factors: a foot of concrete ledge counts for as much as a foot of comfortable bench space. We considered weighting the figures on a point basis—so many points for a foot of bench with backrest, with armrests, and so on. This would have produced a nicer conformance on the chart.

27

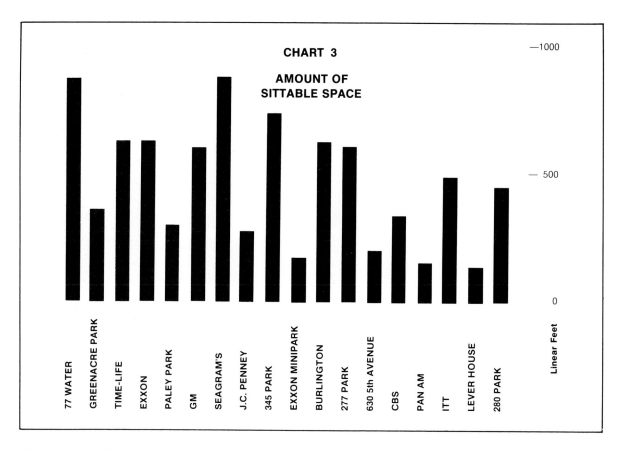

CHART 3

AMOUNT OF
SITTABLE SPACE

—1000

— 500

0

Linear Feet

77 WATER
GREENACRE PARK
TIME-LIFE
EXXON
PALEY PARK
GM
SEAGRAM'S
J.C. PENNEY
345 PARK
EXXON MINIPARK
BURLINGTON
277 PARK
630 5th AVENUE
CBS
PAN AM
ITT
LEVER HOUSE
280 PARK

We gave up the idea, however, as too manipulative. Once you start working backwards this way, there's no end to it.

There was no necessity. No matter how many variables we checked, one point kept coming through. We at last saw that it was the major one:

People tend to sit most where there are places to sit.

This may not strike you as an intellectual bombshell, and, now that I look back on our study, I wonder why it was not more apparent to us from the beginning. Sitting space, to be sure, is only one of the many variables, and, without a control situation as a measure, one cannot be sure of cause and effect. But sitting space is most certainly prerequisite. The most attractive fountains, the most striking designs, cannot induce people to come and sit if there is no place to sit.

Integral Sitting

Ideally, sitting should be physically comfortable—benches with backrests, well-contoured chairs. It's more important, however, that it be *socially* comfortable. This means choice: sitting up front, in back, to the side, in the sun, in the shade, in groups, off alone.

Choice should be built into the basic design. Even though benches and chairs can be added, the best course is to maximize the sittability of inherent features. This means making ledges so they are sittable, or making other flat surfaces do double duty as table tops or seats. There are almost always such opportunities. Because the elevation changes somewhat on most building sites, there are bound to be several levels of flat space. It's no more trouble to make them sittable than not to.

It takes real work to create a lousy place. Ledges have to be made high and bulky; railings put in; surfaces canted. Money can be saved by not doing such things, and the open space is more likely to be an amenable one.

This is one of the lessons of Seagram's. Philip Johnson recounts that when Mies van der Rohe saw people sitting on the ledges, he was quite surprised. He had never dreamt they would. But the architects had valued simplicity. So there were no fussy railings, no shrubbery, no gratuitous changes in elevation, no ornamentation to clutter spaces. The steps were made easy and inviting. The place was eminently sittable, without a bench on it. The periphery includes some 600 feet of ledge and step space, which is just right for sitting, eating, and sunbathing. People use all of it.

So ledges ought to be sittable. But how should this be defined? If we wanted sittable ledges in the New York City zoning amendments we thought we would have to indicate how high or low ledges should

Most ledges are inherently sittable, but with a little ingenuity and additional expense they can be made unsittable.

be, how deep, and, since there were adversary proceedings ahead, be able to back up the specifications with facts.

The proceedings turned out to be adversary in a way we hadn't expected. The attack came on the grounds that the zoning was *too specific*. And it came not from builders, but from members of a local planning board. Rather than spell out the requirements in specific detail, the board argued, the zoning should deal only with broad directives—for example, make the place sittable—leaving details to be settled on a case-by-case basis.

Let me pause to deal with this argument. It is a persuasive one, especially for laymen, and, at the inevitable moment in zoning meetings when someone gets up and says, "Let's cut through all this crap and get down to basics," everyone applauds. Be done with bureaucratic nitpicking and legal gobbledygook.

But ambiguity is a worse problem. Most incentive zoning ordinances are very, very specific as to what the developer gets. The trouble is that they are mushy as to what he is to give, and mushier yet as to what will happen if later he doesn't. Vague stipulations, as many cities have learned, are

unenforceable. What you do not prescribe quite explicitly, you do not get.

Lack of guidelines does not give builders and architects more freedom. It reinforces convention. That is why so few good plazas were built under the 1961 zoning resolution. There was no law preventing builders from providing better plazas. There weren't any guidelines either. And most builders do not do anything far out of the ordinary. A few had sought special permits for amenities not countenanced by existing regulations. But the time-consuming route to obtain special permits makes the builder and architect run a gauntlet of city agencies, with innovation as likely to be punished as rewarded.

Sitting Heights

One guideline we expected to establish easily was the matter of sitting heights. It seemed obvious enough that somewhere around 17 inches would probably be near the optimum. But how much higher or lower could a surface be and still be sittable? Thanks to the slope of sites, several of the most sat-upon ledges provided a

Some places, like Liberty Plaza in Washington, D.C., combine good sitting heights and bad sitting heights.

When ledges are two backsides deep, choice is greatly enlarged and more people can use the ledges without feeling crowded.

range of continuously variable heights. The front ledge of Seagram's, for example, started at 7 inches at one corner, rising to 44 at the other. Here was a dandy chance, we thought, to do a definitive study. By repeated observation, we could record how many people sat at which point over the range of heights; as cumulative tallies built, preferences would become clear.

They didn't. At a given time there might be clusters of people on one part of the ledge, considerably fewer on another. But correlations didn't last. When we cumulated several months of observation, we found that people distributed themselves with remarkable evenness over the whole range of heights. We had to conclude that people will sit almost anywhere between a height of one foot and three, and this is the range specified in the new zoning. People will sit on places higher or lower, to be sure, but there are apt to be special conditions.

Another dimension is more important: the human backside. It is a dimension architects seem to have forgotten. Rarely will you find a ledge or bench deep enough to be sittable on both sides; some aren't deep enough to be sittable on one.

Most frustrating are the ledges just deep enough to tempt people to sit on both sides, but too shallow to let them do so comfortably. Observe such places and you will see people making awkward adjustments. The benches at General Motors plaza are a case in point. They are 24 inches deep and normally used on only one side. On Sundays, however, a heavy influx of tourists and other people will sit on both sides of the benches. Not in comfort: they have to sit on the forward edge, erectly, and their stiff demeanor suggests a tacit truce.

Thus to another of our startling findings: ledges and spaces two backsides deep seat more people comfortably than those that are not as deep. While 30 inches will do it, 36 is better yet. The new zoning provides a good incentive. If a ledge or bench is 30 inches deep and accessible on both sides, the builder gets credit for the linear feet on each side. (The 30-inch figure is thoroughly empirical; it is derived from a ledge at 277 Park Avenue, the minimum-depth ledge we came across that was consistently used on both sides.)

For a few additional inches of depth, then, builders can double the amount of sitting space. This does not mean that

31

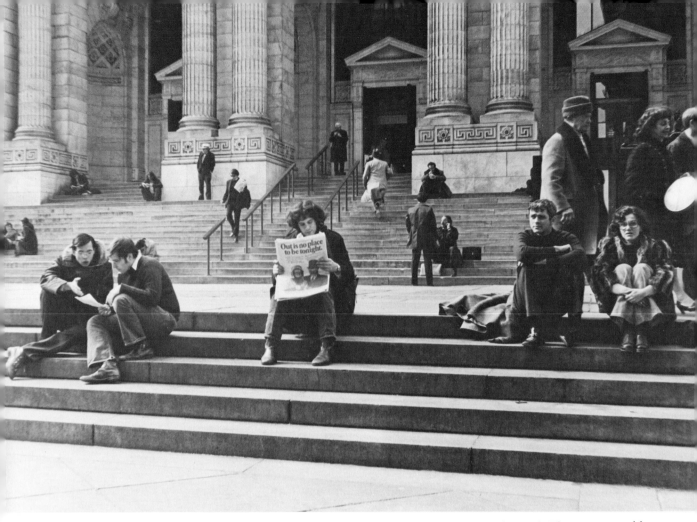

Except on very beautiful days, the steps of the New York Public Library are underused. These steps could become one of New York's great gathering spots.

double the number of people will use the space. They probably won't. But that is not the point. The benefit of the extra space is social comfort—more room for groups and individuals to sort themselves out, more choices and more perception of choices.

Steps work for the same reason. The range of space provides an infinity of possible groupings, and the excellent sightlines make virtually all the seats great for watching the theater of the street. The new zoning ordinance does not credit steps as sitting space. It was felt that this would give builders too easy an out and that some plazas would be all steps and

little else. But the step principle can be applied with good effect to ledges.

Corners are functional. You will notice that people often bunch at the far end of steps, especially when an abutting ledge provides a right angle. These areas are good for face-to-face sitting. People in groups gravitate to them.

One might, as a result, expect a conflict, for corners are also the places where pedestrian traffic is heaviest. Most people take short cuts, and pedestrian flows in plazas are usually on the diagonals between the building entrance and the corners of the steps. We see this at Seagram's. As mentioned previously, the main flow to

and from the building cuts directly across the step corners, and it is precisely there that you will find the heaviest concentration of people sitting, sunbathing, and picnicking. But, for all the bustle, or because of it, the sitters seem to feel comfortable. The walkers don't seem to mind either, and will carefully negotiate through the blockages rather than detour around them.

We find similar patterns at other places. All things being equal, you can calculate that where pedestrian flows bisect a sittable place, that is where people will most likely sit. And it is not so perverse of them. It is by choice that they do. If there is some congestion, it is an amiable one, and a testimonial to the place.

Circulation and sitting, in sum, are not antithetical but complementary. It is to encourage both that the zoning stipulates the plaza not be more than three feet above or below street level. The easier the flow between street and plaza, the more likely people are to move between the two—and to tarry and sit.

This is true of the handicapped, too. If circulation and amenities are planned with them in mind, the place is apt to function more easily for everyone. Drinking fountains that are low enough for wheelchair users are low enough for children. Pedestrian paths that are made easier for the handicapped by ramps, handrails, and steps of gentle pitch are easier for all. The new zoning makes such amenities mandatory, specifying, among other things, that all steps along the main access paths have treads at least 11 inches deep, closed risers no higher than 7.5 inches, and that ramps be provided alongside them. For the benefit of the handicapped, the zoning also requires that at least 5 percent of the seating spaces have backrests. These are not segregated for the handicapped, it should be noted. No facilities are segregated. The idea is to make all of a place usable for everyone.

Benches

Benches are artifacts the purpose of which is to punctuate architectural photographs. They're not so good for sitting. There are too few of them; they are too small; they are often isolated from other benches or from whatever action there is on the plaza. Worse yet, architects tend to repeat the same module in plaza after plaza, unaware that it didn't work very well in the first place. For example, Harrison and Abramowitz's plazas at Rockefeller Center are excellent in many respects, but the basic bench module they've stuck to is exquisitely wrong in its dimensions— 7.5 feet by 19 inches. A larger rectangle would be proportionately as good but work vastly better, as some utilitarian benches in the same area demonstrate.

The technological barriers to better bench design are not insuperable. The prime specification, that benches be generously sized, is the easiest to meet. Backrests and armrests are proved devices. The old-fashioned park bench is still one of the best liked because it provides them; of the newer designs that also do, some of the stock ones of the play- and park-equipment manufacturers are best. Architects have had a way with chairs; for some reason they seem to come a cropper with benches.

They do worst when they freeze their bench designs in concrete permanence. If some of their assumptions prove wrong—that, say, people want to sit away from the action—it will be too late to do much about it. This has been a problem with a number of pedestrian malls, where all design bets were made before the mall was opened. If some of the sitting areas go unused, there's no easy way of heeding the lesson, or, indeed, of recognizing that there is one.

Why not experiment? Some features, like ledges and steps, will be fixed, but benches and chairs don't have to be. With sturdy wooden benches or the like, some simple market research can be done to find out where and in what kind of groupings they work best. People will be very quick to let you know. We have found that by the second day the basic use patterns will be established, and these won't change very much unless the set-up is changed. And it will be clear in what direction the changes should be made.

If one looks. This is the gap. Rarely will you ever see a plan for a public space that even countenances the possibility that parts of it might not work very well: that calls for experiment and testing, and for post-construction evaluation to see what does work well and what doesn't. Existing spaces suffer a similar fate. There are few that could not be vastly improved, but rarely is an evaluation undertaken. The people responsible for the place are the least likely of all to consider it.

Chairs

Now, a wonderful invention—the movable chair. Having a back, it is comfortable; more so, if it has an armrest as well. But the big asset is movability. Chairs enlarge choice: to move into the sun, out of it, to make room for groups, move away from them. The possibility of choice is as important as the exercise of it. If you know you can move if you want to, you feel more comfortable staying put. This is why, perhaps, people so often move a chair a

34

few inches this way and that before sitting in it, with the chair ending up about where it was in the first place. The moves are functional, however. They are a declaration of autonomy, to oneself, and rather satisfying.

Small moves say things to other people. If a newcomer chooses a chair next to a couple or a larger group, he may make some intricate moves. Again, he may not take the chair very far, but he conveys a message. Sorry about the closeness, but there's no room elsewhere, and I am going to respect your privacy, as you will mine. A reciprocal move by one of the others may follow. Watching these exercises in civility is itself one of the pleasures of a good place.

Fixed individual seats are not good.

They are a design conceit. Brightly painted and artfully grouped, they can make fine decorative elements: metal loveseats, revolving stools, squares of stone, sitting stumps. But they are set pieces. That is the trouble with them. Social distance is a subtle measure, ever changing, and the distances of fixed seats do not change, which is why they are rarely quite right for anybody. Loveseats may be all right for lovers, but they're too close for acquaintances, and much too close for strangers. Loners tend to take them over, placing their feet squarely on the other seat lest someone else sit on it.

Fixed seats are awkward in open spaces because there's so much space around them. In theaters, strangers sit next to each other without qualm; the closeness is

Above: Benches at Mechanics Plaza in San Francisco face the action of Market Street.
Left: Benches put right in the middle of the sidewalk outside 747 Third Avenue draw heavy use.

Forced choice is rarely chosen.

a necessity, and convention makes it quite tolerable. On plazas, the closeness is gratuitous. With so much space around, fixed-seat groupings have a manipulative cuteness to them. The designer is saying, now you sit right here and you sit there. People balk. In some instances, they wrench the seats from their moorings. Where there is a choice between fixed seats and other kinds of sitting, it is the other that people choose.

To encourage the use of movable chairs, we recommended that in the zoning amendment they be credited as 30 inches of sitting space, though most are only about 19 inches wide. The Building Department objected. It objected to the idea of movable chairs at all. The department had the responsibility of seeing that builders lived up to requirements. Suppose the chairs were stolen or broken and the builder didn't replace them? Whether the department would ever check up in any event was a moot point, but it was true that the fewer such amenities to monitor, the easier the monitoring would be.

Happily, there was a successful record at

The impulse to move chairs, whether only six or eight inches, is very strong. Even where there is no functional reason for it, the exercise of choice is satisfying. Perhaps this is why the woman above moved her chair a foot—neither into the sun nor out of it.

Paley and Greenacre parks to point to, and it was decisively persuasive. The chairs stayed in. They have become a standard amenity at new places, and the maintenance experience has been excellent. Managements have also been putting in chairs to liven up existing spaces, and, even without incentives, they have been adding more chairs. The most generous provider is the Metropolitan Museum of Art. Alongside its front steps, it puts out up to 200 movable chairs and it leaves them out, 24 hours a day, seven days a week. The Met figured that it might be less expensive to trust people and to buy replacements periodically rather than have guards gather the chairs in every night. That is the way it has worked out. There is little vandalism.

How Much Sitting Space?

A key question we had to confront was how much sitting space should be required. We spent a lot of time on this— much too much, I now realize—and I'm tempted to recount our various calcula-

People outside the Metropolitan Museum of Art move their chairs close to the sidewalk to enjoy the passersby on Fifth Avenue.

tions to demonstrate how conscientious we were. The truth is that almost any reasonable yardstick would work as well as ours. It's the fact of one that is important.

This said, let me tell how conscientious we were. We measured and remeasured the sitting space on most of the plazas and small parks in midtown and downtown New York. As sitting space, we included

Exxon minipark.

all the spaces meant for people to sit on, such as benches, and the spaces they sat on whether meant to or not, such as ledges. Although architects' plans were helpful, we did most of the measuring with a tape, on the ground, in the process

stirring inordinate curiosity from passersby and guards.

Next, we related the amount of sitting space to the size of the plaza. As chart 3 shows, the square feet of sitting space on the best-used plazas ran between 6 and 10 percent of the total open space. As a ball-park figure, it looked like somewhere around 10 percent would be a reasonable minimum to require of builders.

For other comparisons we turned to linear feet. This is a more precise measure of sitting space than square feet, and a more revealing one. As long as there's some clearance for one's back, the additional square inches behind one don't matter very much. It is the edges of sitting surface that do the work, and it is the edges that should be made the most of.

For a basis of comparison, we took the number of linear feet around the total site. Since the perimeter includes the building, the distance is a measure of the bulk of the project and its impact on the surrounding environment. Amenities should therefore be in some proportion to it. On the most popular plazas, there were almost as many feet of sitting space as there were perimeter feet. This suggested that, as a minimum, builders could be asked to provide that amount of sitting space.

Even on the best plazas, the architects could have done better. To get an idea of how much better, we calculated the additional space that could have been provided on various plazas rather easily, while the original plans were being made. We did not posit any changes in basic layout, nor did we take the easy way of adding a lot of benches. We concentrated on spaces that would be integral to the basic design.

In most cases, it was possible to add as much as 50 percent more sitting space, and very good space at that. The Exxon plaza, for example, has a fine pool bordered by two side ledges that you can't sit on. You can sit on the front and back ledges, but only on the sides facing away from the pool. With a few simple changes, such as broadening the ledges, sitting capacity could have been doubled, providing some of the best poolside space anywhere. All in all, these examples indicated, build-

The maximum use of flat surfaces at 345 Park Avenue offers a tremendous choice of sitting combinations.

ers could easily furnish as many feet of sitting space as there are feet around the perimeter of the project.

The requirement finally settled on was a compromise: one linear foot of sitting space for every thirty square feet of plaza. This is reasonable, and builders have been meeting the requirement with no trouble. They could meet a stiffer one. The exact ratio is not as important, however, as the necessity of considering the matter. Once an architect has to start thinking of ways to make a place sittable, it is virtually impossible not to surpass any minimum. And other things follow. More thought must be given to probable pedestrian flows, placement of steps, trees, wind baffles, sun traps, and even wastebaskets. One felicity leads to another. Good places tend to be all of a piece—and the reason can almost always be traced to a human being.

Sun, Wind, Trees, and Water

3

Farragut Square, Washington, D.C.

Sun

The most satisfying film I've ever seen is our first time-lapse record of the sun passing across the Seagram plaza. In late morning, the plaza was in shadow. Then, shortly before noon, a narrow wedge of sunlight began moving across the plaza and, as it did, so did the sitters. Where there was sun, they sat; where there was none, they didn't. It was a perfectly splendid correlation, and I cherished it. Like the urban designers, I believed a southern exposure of critical importance. Here was abundant proof.

Then something went wrong. The correlations vanished—not only at Seagram's but at other places we were studying. The sun still moved; the people didn't. The obvious at length dawned on us: May had been followed by June. While midday temperatures hadn't risen a great deal, the extra warmth was enough to make the sun no longer the critical factor.

It was about this time that much of Paley Park's sunlight began to be cut off by an office building going up across the street. From its scaffolding we focused time-lapse cameras on the park and recorded the effect of the new building. It was surprisingly little. Although the sunlight was curtailed, people used Paley as much as they had before. Perhaps they would have used it more had the sun remained; without an identical place as control, one can never be sure. The more

Left: People enjoy sun.
Below: Sculpture Garden at the Museum of Modern Art.

important point is that, unfortunate as the loss may have been, the park was able to sustain it.

What simple figures don't measure, however, is the quality of the experience, which can be much greater when there is sun. For then you have choice—of sun, or shade, or in-between. The best time to sit beneath a tree is when there is sunlight to be shaded from. The more access to sun, the better, and, if there is a southern exposure, it should be made the most of. New York's zoning now requires that new plazas and open spaces be so oriented.

Access to the sun should be protected. One way of doing so is by acquiring air rights to low buildings across the way, so they will stay low. This can be expensive, very much so if the speculative pressures in the area are rising. For the same reason, however, purchase can prove a good investment. The rights can have a high leverage over subsequent development, and there would be the possibility of selling part of the rights for construction designed to cast minimum shadow on the open space. At present, most air-rights

Above: Sun and grass in the middle of a city make for an enjoyable lunchtime break. *Right:* Some new buildings reflect tremendous amounts of light, often into areas that never got it before.

42

transactions involve purchase of unused rights over one building so that another one can be built higher than normally permissible. It would not be a bad idea to apply the principle the other way around to keep bulk lower than permissible.

On the other hand, there is a good side to our seemingly negative findings about the importance of the sun: places that have little or no sun because of a northern exposure or intervening buildings are not a lost cause. With adroit design, they can be made to seem as if they had sun.

Why not borrow sun? The same new buildings that cast shadows also reflect light in considerable amounts. Along with mirror walls, glass and stainless steel, architects have been laying on travertine with a heavy hand, and their new buildings have sent the glare index of cities soaring. But light has also been bouncing into many places that didn't receive it before. In eight years of filming, I have found that several streets have become photographically a half-stop faster. A number of open spaces that otherwise would be dark much of the time are bathed in reflected light, sometimes on the second or third bounce. Grace plaza, for example, gets no direct sun at all but benefits most of the afternoon from light reflected by the southern exposure of the building to the north. Give travertine its due. It bounces light admirably, especially in the late afternoon, when it can give a benign glow to the streetscape.

So far such effects are wholly inadvertent. Sun studies made for big new buildings tend to be defensive in nature, so that planning boards can be shown the building won't cast an awful lot more shadow than is cast already by other buildings. Few studies try to determine the light a new building will cast, what benefits there might be from it, to whom and when.

Yet benefits of great potential value can be planned and negotiated in advance.

There could be, for example, sun easements, through which, in effect, the developer of a building sells reflected light to neighbors. On an incentive basis, the program could be administered by the city's planning commission, with the developer given bonus points for the benefits reflected. The complexities, of course, might be awesome, but they are the kind of complexities that lawyers and planners involved in urban design find stimulating.

Warmth is just as important as sunlight. The days that bring out the peak crowds on plazas are not the sparkling sunny days with temperatures in the seventies, good as this weather might be for walking. It is the hot, muggy days, sunny or overcast, the kind that could be expected to make people want to stay inside and be air conditioned, when you will find the peak numbers outside. People do like warmth. In summer, they will generally sit in the sun as well as in shade; only in very hot weather—90 degrees or more—will the sunny spots be vacant. Relative warmth is important, too. One of the peak sitting days is the first warm day in spring, even though the same temperature later would be felt too cool for sitting. Similarly, the first warm day after a stretch of cool or rainy days will be a peak day.

Cool weather can be good for sitting, too. It is then that a space open to the radiant heat of the sun's rays can make the difference between sitting comfortably and not sitting at all. People will actively seek the sun and, given the right spots, they will sit in surprising numbers in quite cold weather. The more northern the latitude, the more ardently will they do so.

Wind

What people seek are suntraps. And the absence of winds and drafts are as critical for these as sun. In this respect, small parks, especially those enclosed on three sides, function well. Physically and psychologically, they feel comfortable, and this is one of the reasons why their relative carrying capacity is so high. New York's Greenacre Park has infrared heaters, but they are used only in extremely cold weather. With sun and protection from wind, the park is quite habitable even on nippy days.

Spaces around new buildings are quite another matter. In winter, many are cold and drafty, and even in moderate weather few people will tarry in such places. The errors are of omission. Wind-tunnel tests on models of new buildings are now customary, but they are not made with people much in mind. The tests for the World Trade Center largely determined stresses in the towers, and the structural steel necessary. What the towers themselves might generate in the way of wind, and the effects on people below, apparently were not a matter of much concern.

The effects are, however, quite measurable. It is now well established that very tall, free-standing towers can generate tremendous drafts down their sides. This has in no way inhibited the construction of such towers, with the result, predictably, that some spaces are frequently uninhabitable. At one bank plaza in Seattle the gusts are sometimes so fierce that safety lines must be strung across the plaza to give people something to hang on to. Chicago has the windiest places, not because of the local wind (which isn't really so very much stronger than in other cities), but because the drafts down the sides of the giant John Hancock and Sears towers are macro in force—often so strong as to prevent people from using the plazas, even if they had reason to.

James Marston Fitch, who has done more than any other architect to badger the profession to consider environmental effects, points out that the problem is conceptual, not technical. "Adverse effects are simply ignored, and the outdoor space designed as if for some ideal climate, ever

The steps of St. Thomas Church are a fine example of a suntrap.

sunny and pleasantly warm. Thus [the spaces] fail in their central pretension—that of eliminating gross differences between architectural and urbanistic spaces, of extending in time the areas in which urban life could freely flow back and forth between the two."

Technically, as Fitch points out, we can greatly lengthen the effective season of outdoor spaces. By asking the right questions in sun and wind studies, by experimentation, we can find better ways to hoard the sun, to double its light, or to obscure it, or to cut down breezes in winter and induce them in summer. We can learn lessons in the semiopen niches and crannies that people often seek. Most new urban spaces are either all outdoors or all

45

indoors; more could be done to encourage
inbetweens. With the use of glass canopies
or small pavilions, semioutdoor spaces
could be created that would be usable in
all but the worst weather. They would be
particularly appropriate in rainy cities, like
Seattle and Portland.

Trees

There are all sorts of good reasons for
trees, but for climatic reasons alone we
should press for many more of them, big
ones too, along the sidewalks and open
spaces of the city. New York's new open-
space zoning has sharply stepped-up requirements: developers must provide a
tree for every 25 feet of sidewalk. It must
be at least 3.5 inches in diameter and
planted flush with the ground. In plazas,
trees must be provided in proportion to
the space (for a plaza of 5,000 feet, a
minimum of six trees).

Trees ought to be related much more
closely to sitting spaces than they usually
are. Of the spaces we have studied, by far
the best liked are those affording a good
look at the passing scene and the pleasure
of being comfortably under a tree while
doing so. This provides a satisfying enclosure; people feel cuddled, protected—very
much as they do under the awning of a
street cafe. As always, they'll be cooler,
too.

Unfortunately, guy wires and planting
beds often serve to rule out any sitting;
even if they don't, the fussiness of design
details works to the same effect. Everything is so wired and fenced you can neither get to the tree or sit on what sur-
rounds it. Where large planters are used,
they are generally too high and their rims
too narrow for comfort.

Developers should be encouraged to
combine trees and sitting spaces. They
should also encourage planting trees in
groves. As Paley Park has demonstrated, if
trees are planted closely together, the

46

Left: This office-building plaza in Denver is a simple grassy park with a few trees. It is well liked and makes a nice complement to the plaza of the First of Denver across the street.

Below: A canopy of a few trees can make a high-traffic area feel very comfortable.

overlapping foliage provides a combination of shade and sunlight that is very pleasing. Arbors can do the same.

Water

Water is another fine element, and designers are doing rather well with it. New plazas and parks provide water in all sorts of forms: waterfalls, waterwalls, rapids, sluiceways, tranquil pools, water tunnels, meandering brooks, fountains of all kinds. In only one major respect is something lacking: access.

One of the best things about water is the look and feel of it. I have always thought that the water at Seagram's looked unusually liquid, and I think it's because you know you can splash your hand in it if you are of a mind to. People do it all the time: they stick their hands in it, their toes, and feet, and, if they splash about, some security guard does not come rushing up to say them nay.

But in many places water is only for looking at. Let a foot touch it and a guard will be there in an instant. Not allowed. Chemicals in the water. Danger of contamination. If you let people start touching water, you are told, the next thing they'll start swimming in it. Sometimes they do. The new reflecting pool at the Christian Science Headquarters in Boston is only a few feet deep, but when it first opened many people started using it for wading and even swimming. It was with some difficulty that the pool was put off limits to such activity and reclaimed for its ornamental function.

It's not right to put water before people and then keep them away from it. But this is what has been happening across the country. Pools and fountains are installed, then immediately posted with signs admonishing people not to touch. Equally egregious is the excessive zeal with which many pools are continually emptied, refilled, vacuumed, and cleaned, as though the primary function of them was their maintenance. Grand Old Buckingham Fountain in Chicago's Grant Park has been put off limits with an electrified fence.

Safety is the usual reason given for keeping people away. But there are better ways than electrocution to handle this problem. At the Auditorium Forecourt Fountain in Portland, Oregon, people have been climbing up and down a complex of sluiceways and falls for some six years. It looks dangerous—designer Lawrence Halprin designed it to look dangerous—and, since the day it opened, there have been no serious mishaps. This splendid fountain is an affirmation of trust in

people, and it says much about the good city of Portland.

Another great thing about water is the sound of it. When people explain why they find Paley Park so quiet and restful, one thing they always mention is the waterwall. In fact, the waterwall is quite loud: the noise level is about 75 decibels close by, measurably higher than the level out on the street. Taken by itself, furthermore, the sound is not especially pleasant. I have played tapes to people and asked them what they thought it was. Usually they grimace and say a subway train, trucks on a freeway, or something just as bad. In the park, however, the sound is perceived as quite pleasant. It is white sound and masks the intermittent honks and bangs that are the most annoying aspects of street noise. It also masks conversations. Even though there are many others nearby, you can talk quite loudly to a companion—sometimes you almost have to—and enjoy a feeling of privacy. On the occasions when the waterwall is turned off, a spell is broken, and the place seems nowhere as congenial. Or as quiet.

Water should be accessible, touchable, splashable. It is no longer so at Chicago's Buckingham Fountain (*left*), now protected from people by an electric fence. Shame.

Food

4

One of the big contributors to Seagram plaza's success is Gus, the vendor who can be found day after day, year after year at the corner of Park Avenue and 52nd Street.

If you want to seed a place with activity, put out food. In New York, at every plaza or set of steps with a lively social life, you will almost invariably find a food vendor at the corner and a knot of people around him—eating, shmoozing, or just standing.

Vendors have a good nose for spaces that work. They have to. They are constantly testing the market, and if business picks up in one spot, there will soon be a cluster of vendors there. This will draw more people, and yet more vendors, and sometimes so many converge that pedestrian traffic slows to a crawl. In front of Rockefeller Plaza during the Christmas holidays, we've counted some 15 vendors in a 40-foot stretch (most of them selling hot pretzels).

The civic establishment deplores all this. There are enough ordinances to make it illegal for vendors, licensed or not, to do business at any spot where business is good. Merchants always get on the backs of the police to enforce the ordinances. In midtown and downtown the most frequently observed police activity is giving summonses to food vendors. Sometimes there are sweeps, the police arriving with trucks to haul the vendors away. The confrontations usually draw big crowds who are clearly on the side of the vendors.

And well they should be. By default, the vendors have become the caterers of the city's outdoor life. They flourish because they're servicing a demand not being met by the regular commercial establishment.

Basic food facilities—a snack bar, tables, chairs—
seed a place with activity.

Plazas are particularly parasitic in this respect. Hardly a one has been constructed
that did not involve the demolition of
luncheonettes and restaurants. The vendor thus fills a void, and this can become
quite clear when he is shooed away. A lot
of the life of the space goes with him.

New York City is less puritanical than
some other places. Many cities have ordinances that not only prevent purveying
food outdoors, but eating there as well. If
you ask officials about this, they tell you of
the dreadful things that would happen
were the restrictions lifted—the dangers

of unhealthful food, terrible litter problems, and so on. Partly because of these restrictions, most of the plaza and building complexes constructed during the past 10 years have no provision of any kind for outdoor eating. The few that do have had to do some pioneering. The First National Bank of Chicago, for example, found that even to provide such minimum facilities as a popcorn cart they had to get special dispensation from the city.

Food attracts people who attract more people. We had an excellent opportunity to observe this shill effect through some semicontrolled experiments at a new plaza. At first there was no food. A moderate number of people used the place. At our suggestion, the management put in a food cart. It was an immediate success (a flower cart was not). More people came. A pushcart vendor set up shop on the sidewalk; then another. Business continued to pick up, for all three vendors. Next, the management got the restaurant in the building to open a small outdoor cafe. More people came and yet more—over and above the number who used the cafe.

The optical leverage in these things is tremendous. For basic props, nothing more is needed than several stacks of folding chairs and tables. Spread them out, put up the colored umbrellas, bring on the waitresses, and the customers and visual effect can be stunning. If the cafe makes money, which most do, all the better. But it can be justified for its shill effect alone. The wonder is that there are not more of them.

New buildings and plazas along the Avenue of the Americas displaced many delis and restaurants. This vacuum has now been taken up by a phalanx of food vendors.

The most basic facility is a snackbar. Paley and Greenacre parks both have pass-through counters featuring good food at reasonable prices, and making a moderate profit. Plenty of tables are provided, and people are welcome to bring their own food—wine, too, if they wish. From the street it sometimes looks like a great big party, and if the line of people for the snackbar gets long, the sight will induce passersby to join. Food, to repeat, draws people, and they draw more people.

We proposed that New York's new zoning law make provision of basic food facilities a requirement for all new plazas and parks. The Planning Commission thought this a bit too much, and the final proposals lack the requirement. But food kiosks and other structures that previously would have been counted as obstructions

The built-in snack bar at Greenacre Park.

are specifically encouraged. So are outdoor cafes; up to 20 percent of the open area can be used for such operations. The provisions were also made retroactive to promote the installation of cafes and facilities on existing plazas.

A happy vindication of our recommendations was provided by the city government. It started a cafe. Next to the municipal building there was a big space, St. Andrews Plaza, and the then Deputy Borough President of Manhattan, Jolie Hammer, conceived the idea of an outdoor cafe with ethnic food. She badgered several organizations into donating tables and chairs and got cafes and bakeries from nearby Little Italy to set up booths. Later, she brought in Chinese and soul-food concessions. The operation was a hit from the beginning, with some 500 to 600 people at the peak of the lunch period.

Ms. Hammer also provided a lesson in space use. Instead of distributing the facilities over the large space, she bunched them and, with the tyrant's hand of a good hostess, grouped the tables closely together. As a consequence, people were compressed into meeting one another; waiting in line or weaving their way through the tables, it was difficult not to. Very quickly, the plaza became a great interchange for city government people, and by any index it is one of the most sociable of places. I've never seen so many people striking up conversations, introducing people, saying hellos and goodbyes. If a check is ever made, it would probably show many marriages and children can be traced back to a summer day at St. Andrews Plaza.

The Street

5

Now we come to the key space for a plaza. It is not on the plaza. It is the street. The other amenities we have been discussing are indeed important: sitting space, sun, trees, water, food. But they can be added. The relationship to the street is integral, and it is far and away the critical design factor.

A good plaza starts at the street corner. If it's a busy corner, it has a brisk social life of its own. People will not just be waiting there for the light to change. Some will be fixed in conversation; others, in some phase of a prolonged goodbye. If there's a vendor at the corner, people will cluster around him, and there will be considerable two-way traffic back and forth between plaza and corner.

A corner of Wall Street is a great place for business conversations.

One of New York's best corners is 49th Street and the Avenue of the Americas, alongside the McGraw-Hill Building. This corner has all of the basics: sitting space, a food vendor, and a heavy pedestrian flow, the middle of which is a favorite place for conversations.

Paley Park (*left and below*) is a superb space for many reasons. One of the most important is its cordial relation with the street. The vestibule is used in its own right. The many passersby greatly enjoy the park. Another of New York's most heavily used sitting spaces (*above*) doesn't even have a name. Like Paley, it has an excellent relation to the street. It is virtually a part of it.

The activity on the corner is a great show and one of the best ways to make the most of it is, simply, not to wall it off. A front-row position is prime space; if it is sittable, it draws the most people. Too often, however, it is not sittable and sometimes by an excruciatingly small margin. Railings atop ledges will do it. At the General Motors Building on Fifth Avenue in New York City, for example, the front ledge faces one of the best of urban scenes. The ledge would be eminently sittable if only there weren't a railing atop it, placed exactly five and three-quarter inches in. Another two inches and you could sit comfortably. Canted ledges offer similar difficulties, especially in conjunction with prickly shrubbery.

Another key feature of the street is retailing—stores, windows with displays, signs to attract your attention, doorways, people going in and out of them. Big new office buildings have been eliminating stores. What they have been replacing them with is a frontage of plate glass through which you can behold bank officers sitting at desks. One of these stretches is dull enough. Block after block of them creates overpowering dullness. The Avenue of the Americas in New York has so many storeless plazas that the few remaining stretches of vulgar streetscape are now downright appealing.

As a condition of an open-space bonus, developers should be required to devote at least 50 percent of the ground-floor frontage to retail and food uses, and the new New York City zoning so stipulates. Market pressures, fortunately, are now working to the same end. At the time of our study, banks were outbidding stores for ground-level space. Since then, the banks have been cutting back, and economics have been tipping things to stores. But it does not hurt to have a requirement.

The area where the street and plaza or open space meet is a key to success or failure. Ideally, the transition should be such that it's hard to tell where one ends and the other begins. New York's Paley Park is the best of examples. The sidewalk in front is an integral part of the park. An arborlike foliage of trees extends over the sidewalk. There are urns of flowers at the curb and, on either side of the steps, curved sitting ledges. In this foyer, you can usually find somebody waiting for someone else—it is a convenient rendezvous point—people sitting on the ledges, and, in the middle of the entrance, several people in conversations.

Passersby are users of Paley, too. About half will turn and look in. Of these, about half will smile. I haven't calculated a smile index, but this vicarious, secondary enjoyment is extremely important—the sight of the park, the knowledge that it is there, becomes part of the image we have of a much wider area. (If one had to make a cost-benefit study, I think it would show that secondary use provides as much, if not more, benefit than the primary use. If one could put a monetary value on a minute of visual enjoyment and multiply that by instances day after day, year after year, one would obtain a rather stupendous sum.)

The park stimulates impulse use. Many people will do a double take as they pass by, pause, move a few steps, then, with a slight acceleration, go on up the steps. Children do it more vigorously, the very young ones usually pointing at the park and tugging at their mothers to go on in, many of the older ones breaking into a run just as they approach the steps, then skipping a step or two.

Watch these flows and you will appreciate how very important steps can be. The steps at Paley are so low and easy that one is almost pulled to them. They add a nice ambiguity to your movement. You can stand and watch, move up a foot, another, and, then, without having made a conscious decision, find yourself in the park.

New York's Bryant Park is dangerous. It has become the territory of dope dealers and muggers because it was relatively underused by other people. Bryant Park is cut off from the street by walls, fences, and shrubbery. You can't see in. You can't see out. There are only a few entry points. This park will be used by people when it is opened up to them.

The steps at Greenacre Park and at Seagram's plaza are similarly low and inviting.

A slight elevation, then, can be beckoning. Go a foot or so higher, however, and usage will fall off sharply. There is no set cut-off level—it is as much psychological as physical—but it does seem bound up with how much of a choice the steps require. One plaza that people could be expected to use, but don't, is only a foot or so higher than two comparable ones nearby. It seems much higher. The steps are constricted in width, sharply defined by railings, and their pitch is brisk. No ambiguity here; no dawdling; no drifting up.

Sightlines are important. If people do not see a space, they will not use it. In the center of Kansas City is a park just high enough above eye level that most passersby do not realize it is there. As a result, it's lost. Similarly lost is a small,

sunny plaza in Seattle. It would be excellent and likely quite popular for sitting—if people could see it from the street, which they cannot.

Unless there is a compelling reason, an open space shouldn't be sunk. With two or three notable exceptions, sunken plazas are dead spaces. You find few people in them; if there are stores, there are apt to be dummy window displays to mask the vacancies. Unless the plaza is on the way to the subway, why go down into it? Once there, you feel rather as if you were at the bottom of a well. People look at you. You don't look at them.

One of the best students of spaces I know is the dancer Marilyn Woods. With her troupe, she has staged stunning "celebrations" of public places across the country. These celebrations are an intensification of the natural choreography of a place. The best places, not too surprisingly, make for the best performances, the most appreciative audiences. (Seagram's and Cincinnati's Fountain Square are at the top of the list.) Significantly, the only places where her celebrations didn't work were sunken plazas. They felt dead, Woods recalls, as if a wall had been put between the dancers and the audience.

What about Rockefeller Plaza? It is a very successful place, and it has a sunken plaza in the middle. So it has. Those who cite it, however, are usually unaware of how it works. The plaza is a great urban space, but the lower plaza is only one part, and it is not where most of the people are. They are in the tiers of an amphitheater. The people in the lower plaza provide the show. In winter, there is skating; in summer, an open-air cafe and frequent concerts. The great bulk of the people—usually about 80 percent—are up above: at the railings along the street, along the mezzanine level just below, or on the broad walkway heading down from Fifth Avenue.

What gets copied? Some cities have dug near facsimiles of Rockefeller Center's lower plaza, in one case to the exact dimensions of the skating rink. What they haven't copied is the surrounding space. They wind up having a stage without a theater, a hole without the doughnut. And they wonder what went wrong.

The plaza of the First National Bank of Chicago is also quite sunken—some 18 feet below street level. And it is the most popular plaza in the country, with well over 1,000 people at lunchtime on a nice day. It is successful because just about everything has been done to make it successful—there is plenty of sitting space, a splendid outdoor cafe, a fountain, murals by Chagall, and usually music and entertainment of some kind at lunchtime.

The First National Bank plaza has an excellent relationship to the street. The sidewalks are part of its space, and there is a strong secondary use by the thousands who pass by. Many pause to look at what's going on. Some will drift down a few steps, then a few more. Again, an amphitheater—with several tiers of people looking at people who are looking at people who are looking at the show.

The sunken plaza of 1633 Broadway.
Don't.

The "Undesirables"

6

If good places are so felicitous, why are there not more of them? The biggest single reason is the problem of "undesirables." They are not themselves much of a problem. It is the measures taken to combat them that is the problem. Many businessmen have an almost obsessive fear that if a place is attractive to people it might be attractive to undesirable people. So it is made unattractive. There is to be no loitering—what a Calvinist sermon is in those words!—no eating, no sitting. So it is that benches are made too short to sleep on, that spikes are put in ledges; most important, many needed spaces are not provided at all, or the plans for them scuttled.

Who are the undesirables? For most businessmen, curiously, it is not muggers, dope dealers, or truly dangerous people. It is the winos, derelicts who drink out of half-pint bottles in paper bags—the most harmless of the city's marginal people, but a symbol, perhaps, of what one might become but for the grace of events. For retailers, the list of undesirables is considerably more inclusive; there are the bag women, people who act strangely in public, "hippies," teenagers, older people, street musicians, vendors of all kinds.

The preoccupation with undesirables is a symptom of another problem. Many corporation executives who make key decisions about the city have surprisingly little acquaintance with the life of its streets and open spaces. From the train station, they

may walk only a few blocks before entering their building; because of the extensive services within the building, some don't venture out until it's time to go home again. To them, the unknown city is a place of danger. If their building has a plaza, it is likely to be a defensive one that they will rarely use themselves.

Few others will either. Places designed with distrust get what they were looking for and it is in them, ironically, that you will most likely find a wino. You will find winos elsewhere, but it is the empty places they prefer; it is in the empty places that they are conspicuous—almost as if, unconsciously, the design was contrived to make them so.

Fear proves itself. Highly elaborate defensive measures are an indicator that a corporation might clear out of the city entirely. Long before Union Carbide announced it was leaving New York for suburbia, its building said it would. Save for an exhibit area, the building was sealed

The plaza of the New York Telephone Company's building at 42nd Street and the Avenue of the Americas was used by "undesirables." New York Telephone's president, John R. Mulhearn, wanted people to enjoy the plaza, and he decided to liven the place up by putting in chairs, tables, and a buffet. It was an immediate success. Employees and passersby enjoy it. Most of the undesirables have gone somewhere else.

off from the city with policelike guards and checkpoints, and in all the empty space around it there was not a place to sit. (There is no surcease in suburbia, it should be noted. Most of the firms that have moved still seem every bit as obsessed with security. New headquarters are often designed like redoubts, with gatehouses, moats, and, in one case, a hillside motor entrance with a modern version of a portcullis.)

The best way to handle the problem of undesirables is to make a place attractive to everyone else. The record is overwhelmingly positive on this score. With few exceptions, plazas and smaller parks in most central business districts are probably as safe a place as you can find during the times that people use them.

The way people use a place mirrors expectations. Seagram's management is pleased people like its plaza and is quite relaxed about what they do. It lets them stick their feet in the pool; does not look to see if kids are smoking pot on the pool ledge; tolerates oddballs, even allowing them to sleep the night on the ledge. The sun rises the next morning. The place is largely self-policing, and there is rarely trouble of any kind.

Paley Park is courtly to people. With its movable chairs and tables, it should be quite vulnerable to vandalism. Here is the record of security infractions at the park since it opened in 1967:

1968. One of the flower urns on the sidewalk was stolen by two men in a van.
1970. The "Refreshments" sign was taken from the wall.
1971. A small table was taken.
1972. A man attempted to carve his initials in one of the trees.
1974. One of the brass lights at the entrance was removed.

In the nine years I have been studying plazas and small parks in New York City,

there has been a serious problem in only one, and in the places that are well used, none at all. The exception is a plaza on which pot dealers began operating. The management took away about half the benches. Next, it constructed steel-bar fences on the two open sides of the plaza. These moves effectively cut down the number of ordinary people who used the place, to the delight of the pot dealers, who now had it much more to themselves and their customers.

At many plazas you will see TV surveillance cameras. What they see is a question. For monitoring remote passageways and doors, the cameras can be useful. For outdoor areas, they don't make very much sense. Occasionally, you will see one move from side to side, and it's rather spooky if it's you that the lens seems to be tracking. But it's probably all in play. Down in the

63

control room, some guard is likely twiddling the dials more out of boredom than curiosity.

Electronics can't beat a human being, and it is characteristic of well-used places to have a "mayor." He may be a building guard, a newsstand operator, or a food vendor. Watch him, and you'll notice people checking in during the day—a cop, bus dispatcher, various street professionals, and office workers and shoppers who pause briefly for a salutation or a bit of banter. Plaza mayors are great communication centers, and very quick to spot any departure from normal. Like us. When we go to a place and start observing—unobtrusively, we like to think—the regulars find us sticking out like sore thumbs. For one thing, we're not moving. Someone will come over before long and find out just what it is we're up to.

One of the best mayors I've seen is Joe Hardy of the Exxon Building. He is an actor, as well as the building guard, and was originally hired by Rockefeller Center Inc. to play Santa Claus, whom he resembles. Ordinarily, guards are not supposed to initiate conversations, but Joe Hardy is gregarious and curious and has a nice sense of situations. There are, say, two older people looking somewhat confused. He will not wait for them to come up and ask for directions. He will go up to them and ask whether he can help. Or, if two girls are taking turns snapping pictures of each other, he may offer to take a picture of the two of them together.

Joe is quite tolerant of winos and odd people, as long as they don't bother anybody. He is very quick to spot real trouble, however. Teenage groups are an especial challenge. They like to test everybody—with the volume knob of their portable radios as weapon. Joe's tactic is to go up to the toughest-looking person in the group and ask his help in keeping things cool.

Unlike Joe Hardy, guards at most places are an underused asset. Usually, they just stand, and for want of anything else to do tend to develop occupational tics. One might wave his arms rhythmically to and fro, or rock up and down on his heels. Another may bend his knees at odd intervals. If you watch, you'll get mesmerized trying to anticipate when the next bend will come. The guard's job ought to be upgraded.

The more a guard has to do, the better he does it, and the better the place functions. At Paley Park it was originally expected that special security guards would be needed, in addition to several people to keep the place tidy and run the snack bar. The two men who worked at keeping the place tidy, however, did such an excellent job that no security guards were needed. Similarly, the guards take a proprietary pleasure in Greenacre Park. They are hosts, friendly to everyone, especially to the regulars, who serve as a kind of adjunct force. If someone flouts one of the unposted rules—like wheeling in a bicycle—it is likely as not the regulars who will set him straight.

Property Rights

Let us turn to a related question. How public are the public spaces? On many plazas you will see a small bronze plaque that reads something like this: PRIVATE PROPERTY. CROSS AT THE RISK OF THE USER AND WITH REVOCABLE PERMISSION OF THE OWNER. It seems clear enough. It means that the plaza is the owner's, and he has the right to revoke any right you may have to use it. Whether or not a floor-area bonus was given, most building managements take it for granted that they can bar activity they believe undesirable. Their definition of this, furthermore, goes beyond dangerous or antisocial behavior. Some are quite persnickety. When we were measuring the front ledges by the sidewalk at the General Motors Building,

Joe Hardy (*left*) helps make the Exxon plaza inviting. Plaques like the one above convey a different message.

the security people rushed up in great consternation; we would have to desist unless we could secure permission from public relations.

This is not one to go to the Supreme Court on, perhaps, but there is principle involved, and inevitably it is going to be tested. The space was really provided by the public—through its zoning and planning machinery. It is true that the space falls within the property line of the developer, and it is equally true that he is liable for the proper maintenance of it. But the zoning legislation enabling the bonus unequivocally states as a condition that the plaza "must be accessible to the public at all times."

What does "accessible" mean? A commonsense interpretation would be that the public could use the space in the same manner as it did any public space, with the same freedoms and the same constraints. Many building managements have

been operating with a much narrower concept of accessibility. They shoo away entertainers, people who distribute leaflets, or give speeches. Apartment building managements often shoo away everybody except residents. This is a flagrant violation of the zoning intent, but to date no one has gone to court.

The public's right in urban plazas would seem clear. Not only are plazas used as public spaces, in most cases the owner has been specifically, and richly, rewarded for providing them. He has not been given the right to allow only those public activities he happens to approve of. He may assume he has, and some owners have been operating on this basis with impunity. But that is because nobody has challenged them. A stiff, clarifying test is in order.

Effective Capacity
7

So far, we have been considering ways of making city spaces attract more people. Now let us turn to another question. What if we were to succeed too well? Conceivably, so many people might be attracted as to crowd out the values they came to enjoy. It has happened at national parks; it could certainly happen in the city. This possibility concerned the New York City Planning Commission. Could our studies shed some light? Was there a way of gauging the carrying capacity of city spaces? Or regulating it? How many people is too many?

To get at the questions, we undertook close-up studies of five of the most intensively used sitting places in New York: a ledge alongside a building, a ledge at a plaza, and three groups of benches. First, we recorded the average number of people sitting at each spot at peak and off-peak hours. It was quickly apparent that the number who could sit and the number who did were quite different. At the highest-used places, we found, the range was between 33 and 38 people per hundred feet of sitting space. In later observations, we noted a slight increase in usage, though the range was about the same as it was in other comparable places we studied. There is thus enough consistency on which to base the following rough rule of thumb: if you wish to estimate the average number of people who will be using a prime sitting space at peak periods, divide

Greenacre Park is one of the most heavily used of spaces—but rarely by so many people as to make it feel crowded.

the number of feet in it by three and you won't be far off from a good figure.

This is not physical capacity. Were people to sit at the same density as they do in buses, the average could go as high as 60 people per 100 feet. In special situations—like an outstanding event—the number can go even higher. What we are concerned with, however, is effective capacity; that is, the number of people who by free choice will sit at a place during normal peak-use periods. Each place, you will find, has its own norm, and it depends on many particulars—the microclimate, the comfort of the perch, what you see from it, the overall attractiveness of the area.

Supply is a major factor. A lot of people have to pass by to provide a quota of sitters; thus there is bound to be a relationship between the use of a sitting place and pedestrian flow. In his studies of Copenhagen, Jan Gehl found a strong correlation between the number of people sitting on benches along the city's main pedestrian way and the number standing or walking. The number sitting was a rather constant fraction of those standing or walking.

Of all factors, of course, the sitters themselves are most important. We concentrated on the north front ledge at Seagram's for a minute-by-minute study of their behavior. From a rooftop across the street we focused two time-lapse cameras on the ledge and at 10-second intervals recorded what went on from early morning to dusk. I used the film to construct a chronological chart, which looks rather like a player piano roll. Each line represents a sitter; the length of the line, the time he spent sitting; the channel that the line is in denotes on which of 11 squares he sat. Each square is four feet eight inches wide; the total ledge, 51 feet. The continuous line at the bottom of the chart shows the total number of sitters at any one time (see pp. 70–71).

The day at Seagram's starts slowly. At 8:50 three people sit down; soon they leave. From then until about 11:30, the total number of people at any one time fluctuates between two and five. A sudden upswing at 10:35 is caused by 26 school children who stop to rest. But it is around 11:30 that the tempo really picks up. Shortly after noon, the number of sitters is up to 18.

When a space begins to fill up, people don't distribute themselves evenly over it; they go where other people are. At Seagram's, the corner of the steps is where the buildup often begins. And the dense areas get denser.

You can see the same phenomenon at beaches. On a busman's holiday in Spain, I set up a time-lapse camera on a bluff overlooking a small beach. When the first comers arrived with their umbrellas, most went to the front and center. As others came, they did not veer off to the empty spaces. Instead, in checkerboard fashion, they located themselves about one or two spaces removed from the other people. By noon the pattern was complete. Beach umbrellas were laid out in three parallel lines and so equispaced you'd think they were laid down by a surveyor. The sides and the rear of the beach were still almost empty.

Even in very high-density places there is the same tendency to cluster. In an excellent study for the National Park Service, the Project for Public Spaces recorded the beach patterns at Jacob Riis Park in New York. On peak-use days as well as others, the film record shows, people will cluster up front rather than fill up the relatively unused areas at the rear. Income levels don't seem to have much to do with this phenomenon. At the other end of Long Island, at the Hamptons, there is a lot more beach available per person, but here, too, the clustering patterns are much the same.

To get back to the Seagram's ledge, as lunchtime gets under way, there will be a

Camera setup for *A Day in the Life of the North Front Ledge at Seagram's* before the people arrive.

group at the steps; the total number on the ledge will be between 18 and 21. It will stay at that for the whole lunch period.

This is an extraordinarily uniform number considering the heavy turnover. For two hours hardly a minute goes by without someone getting up or sitting down. Yet the overall number will fluctuate only slightly. Whenever it reaches 21, almost immediately someone will get up and leave. If it drops to 18, someone will sit down. A self-regulating factor seems to be at work.

Good spacing, one might assume. To a point, yes, but this doesn't really explain matters. Note that at no time during the peak hours are people evenly spaced over the ledge, like starlings on a telephone wire, nor do those who leave do so because they personally are crowded. In

some places, there will be clumps of people sitting closely together; elsewhere, people have considerable space around them. This is true even at the three peak moments—12:50, 1:25, and 1:50. There are enough spaces to take care of another half-dozen people easily.

But they do not appear. It's as if people had some instinctive sense of what is right overall for a place and were cooperating to maintain it that way, obligingly leaving, or sitting down, or not sitting, to keep the density within range. Happenstance is at work, too—the four friends who squeeze into a space left by three, the chance succession of three loners. But, over time, happenstance can be quite regular.

Whatever the mechanism, there seems to be a norm that influences people's choices as much as the immediate physical space. Thus is effective capacity determined. It is not static; nor can it be expressed only in figures. And there are qualitative aspects to consider—whether people are comfortable, leave quickly or tarry—that can be quite different for different people.

There may even be music of sorts. Note the up-tempo flurry of dashes around 10 minutes to 2:00. This is a recurrent motif. It's up tempo on the ground, too: the last-minute return of late lunchers. Since the Seagram's chart looked so like a player-piano roll, I wondered what the sound would be if all the dots and dashes could be played. A composer friend was fascinated: with the right tonal scale, he said, the roll could be orchestrated and it would be music. I hope one day it will be: *A Day in the Life of the North Front Ledge at Seagram's, Adagio.*

The most intensively used places we have found are benches on the islands in the middle of upper Broadway. Environmentally, these places are awful. There is maximum traffic noise and fumes from the adjacent roadways; the sound of the subway emerges from below; the benches

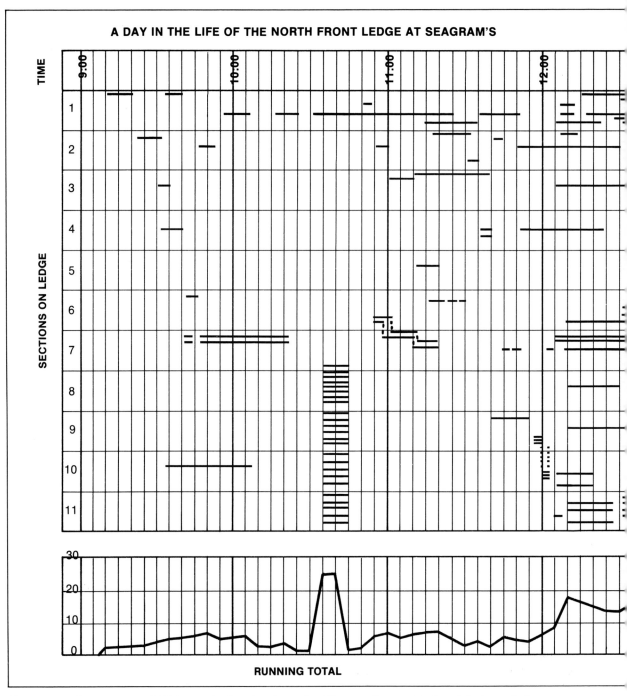

A DAY IN THE LIFE OF THE NORTH FRONT LEDGE AT SEAGRAM'S

How many is too many? This analysis of a day of sitting at the north front ledge of the Seagram plaza indicates that in their instinctive way people have a nice sense of what is right for a place. Plan view shows 11 sections of ledge at left. The lines going from left to right show on which part of the ledge each person sat and precisely how long. Morning activity is desultory. (The sharp upswing at 10:35 is due to 25 school children.) At noon, activity picks up

70

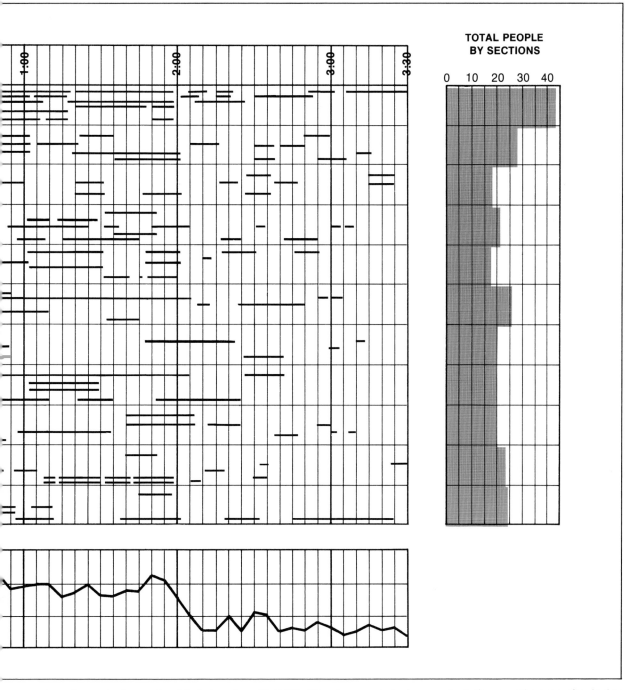

TOTAL PEOPLE
BY SECTIONS

0   10   20   30   40

sharply and stays at a high level until 2:00. The turnover is heavy, but the number on the ledge at any time stays remarkably uniform—as running total at bottom shows, between 18 and 21 people. The number is not constricted by lack of space. Note that at the peak-use moments, there is plenty of space for more sitters. But they don't appear. In free-choice situations such as this, evidently, capacity tends to be self-leveling, and people determine it rather effectively.

71

are dilapidated, and often draped with derelicts and dope addicts. But to older people in the area these places are precious. In mid-afternoon each 18-foot bench will have between seven and nine people sitting on it. Per hundred feet, this is a very high range, between 39 and 50. Interestingly, the highest densities can be found at the major crosstown streets, where there is the most noise and pollution—as well as the most action to look at.

Our sitting chart of Seagram's yields several other points worth noting. One is the uniformity with which the *total* number of sitters is distributed along the ledge. At any one time there is little uniformity. By the end of the day, however, the cumulative totals for each of the ledge's 11 squares are similar. There is one exception: the square next to the

steps. It has two edges and attracts double the number of sitters.

The log of the amount of time people sit is also revealing. Because of the high turnover, it is easy to assume that in-and-outers account for the bulk of the time spent on the ledge. But appearances are deceptive. Over the day charted at Seagram's there were some 266 sitters. And, as might be expected, the number who stayed for a few minutes was greater than the number who stayed longer. Add up the total amount of time spent sitting, however, and you find that those who stayed longer logged by far the most of it. Of the total—some 3,277 minutes—about three quarters was logged by people staying 11 minutes or more; almost half by those staying 21 minutes or more. A study of the south ledge showed similar results;

Benches on a traffic island in the middle of upper Broadway.

72

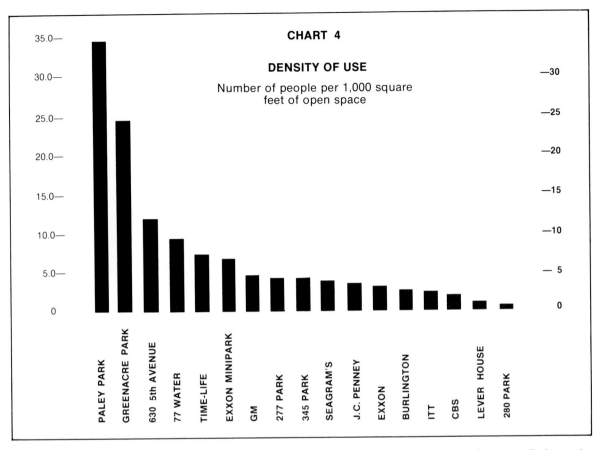

CHART 4

DENSITY OF USE

Number of people per 1,000 square
feet of open space

35.0—
30.0—   —30
25.0—   —25
20.0—   —20
15.0—   —15
5.0—   — 5
0   0

PALEY PARK
GREENACRE PARK
630 5th AVENUE
77 WATER
TIME-LIFE
EXXON MINIPARK
GM
277 PARK
345 PARK
SEAGRAM'S
J.C. PENNEY
EXXON
BURLINGTON
ITT
CBS
LEVER HOUSE
280 PARK

The two places people cite as the most pleasing, least crowded in New York—Paley Park and Greenacre Park—are by far and away the most heavily used per square foot. This is immensely encouraging, for it demonstrates how great is the carrying capacity of urban space, given a sensitive design.

three quarters of the time spent on the ledge during lunch hours was accounted for by people staying 15 minutes or more. There is a lesson here for designers: design for the person who's going to sit awhile.

Capacity, to recapitulate, is self-leveling. This is a point that needs to be made over and over. Many planning boards worry about carrying capacity and fear that more amenities, more sitting spaces, could stimulate too much use, more pedestrian congestion. But it is the obverse that they should be worrying about. Underuse, not overuse, is the major problem. The carrying capacity of most urban open spaces is far above the use that is made of them,

and the lesson of the exceptions is encouraging. The places that carry the most people are the most efficient in the use of space as well as the most pleasant. It is people who determine the level of crowding, and they do it very well.

It was with this in mind, as well as the lessons noted in previous chapters, that New York's excellent Urban Design Group pulled together various guidelines into a proposed zoning amendment. We had expected the issue to be akin to motherhood and the flag. And so it was with some groups, like the Municipal Art Society and the New York chapter of the American Institute of Architects. They demurred a bit over specifics, but gave strong support.

The zoning proved surprisingly controversial, however, with local planning boards. As a result, one of the best provisions was sacrificed—the small park bonus. This would have meant that instead of building a plaza a developer could get his additional floor space by providing a small Paley-type park on a side street nearby. It would have to be a good park, with plenty of seating, food facilities, trees, and the like. The developer would have to maintain it and post a performance bond. The small park bonus would have been a good deal for all concerned: the developer would get land at side street prices and multiply it into avenue floor space; the city at no cost would get a park, and this might be far more of an amenity to people in the area than yet another plaza. Unhappily, one local planning board fought the idea, and, to get its support for the rest of the zoning package, the City Planning Commission cut out the small park option. The local board fought the package anyway.

After an interminable series of meetings and presentations with various groups, the zoning amendment went before the city's Board of Estimate, and, in May 1975, was adopted by unanimous vote. This was just in time for the collapse of the building boom, and it was to be some time before the new guidelines appeared in brick and mortar. But the hiatus was useful. The Urban Design Group drafted companion guidelines for residential buildings, calling for neighborhood parks instead of the fenced-off spaces developers had been getting away with. The new guidelines were incorporated into the zoning code in December 1977.

The consequences have been encouraging. It may be that you can't legislate good design, but it certainly helps to have some directives on the official books. Now the easy, normal, quickest way for builders is to plan on providing generous spaces with trees and chairs and cafes, and with little

fuss or complaint builders have been doing this, happily patting themselves on the back. The new zoning has not only set standards for plazas, but, in effect, for other kinds of spaces, such as atriums, or indoor parks, and some imaginatively designed ones are coming along. One thing does lead to another, and the examples of the best new places have obviously stirred competitive instincts in a number of corporations.

The amenities have proved so demonstrably worthwile as to pose a question. Is it necessary to give so much floor-space bonus to get them? What has been increasingly troubling the planning boards, and with good reason, is the *bulk* of new buildings. They are bigger than the zoning had anticipated, but they are bigger because of the zoning. Taken one by one, the special floor area bonuses that have periodically been added to the zoning have made sense. The trouble is that builders have been combining them into a whole that the parts weren't meant to add up to. This fact, furthermore, is reflected in the market price of land, and, as developers are quick to plead, this forces them to seek the maximum permissible bulk.

Then there is the increasing use of air-

74

rights transfer. The basic idea is good and has been well applied to the protection of landmarks. But it does provide another upward push. By combining every feasible bonus provision with a purchase of air rights from a nearby site, the developer can put up a building with a floor area ratio (f.a.r.) of up to 21.6—versus the nominal 15 originally stipulated.

And there is not much that planning boards can do about it. True, none of the big new buildings have been per se "as of right"; they are so complicated, require special permits, that all of them have been subject to extensive review by the various boards. During these sessions, boards customarily push for additional amenities and design improvements from the developer, and he is likely to grant them, if only to buy his way out of another marathon session. But on one matter, he won't yield: bulk. He doesn't have to. Each of the components of the various bonuses is "as of right," and, if they add up to 21.6 f.a.r., that is it. The law says so.

As a consultant on the open spaces of two of the biggest new buildings, those of AT&T and Philip Morris, I must note a bias. I think these spaces should work very well for the people, for the neighboring buildings, and fully justify the additional floor area. So, too, should some other new spaces, such as IBM's.

But how many is too many? And where? The problem is not the individual buildings so much as their growing number and proximity. Not only are there more very big buildings, they are being clustered in the highest-density areas rather than in less built-up areas. Then there is the matter of what they are displacing. By allowing much bigger buildings in particular districts, the zoning seems to be inducing the destruction of some good old buildings that otherwise would remain economic.

The New York City Planning Commission has embarked on a major review of incentive zoning, and this is likely to lead to a tightening of density and bulk limits. In the meantime, the marketplace is giving a partial answer to one question. For enlightened self-interest, owners can be induced to provide amenities, for their own sake.

Though they receive no bonus for it, the revised open-space zoning has spurred owners to re-do their existing plazas. Some very pleasant and well-used places have been the result. The Exxon mini-park, which had its problems for a while, is one of the best. On the basis of an analysis by the Project for Public Spaces, it was completely made over into a sort of food and music garden, with clusters of chairs and tables, and two snack bars. At lunch, jazz groups play. The place is busy with people.

At other places, food facilities are being provided, more trees planted, and more seating is being installed, not only on plazas but on sidewalks, in front of stores, alongside bus stops and odds and ends of space. This is taking place in other cities, too, but on one point I must take parochial pride. Whatever else it may be, New York is now incontestably the most sittable city in the country.

Indoor Spaces 8

As an alternative to plazas, builders have been turning to indoor spaces. There are many variants: atriums, galleries, courtyards, through-block arcades, indoor parks, covered pedestrian areas of one shape or another. Some are dreadful. In return for extra floors, the developers provided spaces and welshed on the amenities. But some spaces have been very successful indeed, and there is enough of a record to indicate that the denominators are much the same as with outdoor spaces. Here, briefly, are the principal needs:

1. *Sitting.* Movable chairs are best for indoor parks. Most of the popular places have had excellent experience with them; some places, like Citicorp, have been adding to the numbers. In all cases the total amount of sitting space has met or exceeded the minimum recommended for outdoor spaces—one linear foot for every 30 square feet of open space. There is a tendency, however, to overlook the potentials of ledges and planters. Too many are by inadvertence lower or higher than need be.

2. *Food.* Every successful indoor space provides food. The basic combination is snack bars and chairs and tables. Some places feature cafe operations as well.

3. *Retailing.* Shops are important for liveliness and the additional pedestrian flows they attract. Developers, who can

Above: The IDS Center in Minneapolis is heavily used throughout the day by people—including those who don't have enough money to drive cars. *Right:* Psychologically as well as visually, the Center has an excellent relationship with the street and surroundings. They are eminently visible, and this helps make pedestrian flows easy.

Market Street entrance of The Gallery in Philadelphia. This enclosed space links two department stores and is an attraction in itself. As with the IDS Center, it does not turn a blank wall to the street, but invites the street in.

often do better renting the space for banks or offices, are not always keen on including shops. They should be required to.

4. *Toilets.* If incentive zoning achieved nothing else, an increase in public toilets would justify it. Thanks to beneficent pressure, new indoor parks in New York are providing a pair or more, uni-sex-style as on airplanes. These facilities are modest, but their existence could have a considerable effect on the shopping patterns of many people, older ones especially.

One benefit of an indoor space is the through-block circulation it can provide for pedestrians. Planners believe this important, and developers have been allowed a lot of additional floor space in return for it. But walking space is about all that some developers have provided, and it has proved no bargain. Unless there are attractions within, people don't use walkways very much, even in rainy or cold weather. The street is a lot more interesting. At New York's Olympic Towers, which is taller by several million dollars worth of extra space for providing a through-block passage, the number of people traversing the passage is about 400 per hour at peak. On the Fifth Avenue sidewalk that parallels the passage, the flow is about 4,000 per hour.

Not so paradoxically, the walk-through function of a space is greatly enhanced if something is going on within it. Even if one does not tarry to sit or get a snack, just seeing the activity makes a walk more interesting. Conceivably, there could be conflict between uses. Planners tend to fret over this and, to ensure adequate separation, they specify wide walkways—in New York, 20 feet at the minimum. But this is more than enough. As at plazas, the places people like best for sitting are those next to the main pedestrian flow, and for many conversations the very middle of the flow. Walkers like the proximity, too. It makes navigation more challenging. At places where there is a multiplicity of flows, as at the IDS Center in Minneapolis, one often gets blocked by people just standing or talking, while there are others in crossing patterns or collision courses up ahead. The processional experience is all the better for the busyness.

In an important respect, public spaces that are inside differ from public spaces that are outside. They're not as public. The look of a building, its entrances, the guards do have a filtering effect and the cross section of the public that uses the space within is somewhat skewed—with more higher-income people, fewer lower-income people, and, presumably, fewer undesirables. This, of course, is just what the building management and shop owners want. But there is a question of equity posed. Should the public underwrite such spaces? In a critique of the Citicorp Building, Suzanne Stephens argues in *Progressive Architecture* that it should not. The suburban shopping mall, she notes, is frankly an enclave and "owes its popularity to what it keeps out as well as what it offers within. Whether this isolationism should occur in 'public spaces' created through the city's incentive zoning measures should be addressed at the city planning level. . . . Open space amenities are moving from the true public domain, the street, to inner sanctums where public and private domains blur. Thus this public space is becoming increasingly privatized."

This is very much the case with most megastructures. They are exclusionary by design, and, as I will argue later, they are wrongly so. But buildings with indoor spaces can be quite hospitable if they are designed to be so, even rather large ones. The Crystal Court of the IDS Center is the best indoor space in the country, and it is used by a very wide mix of people. In mid-morning, the majority of the people sitting and talking are older people, and many of them are obviously of limited means.

Inevitably, any internal space is bound to have a screening effect; its amenities, the merchandise lines offered, the level of the entertainment—all these help determine the people who will choose to come, and it is not necessarily a bad thing if a good many of the people are educated and well-off. But there should be other kinds of people, too, and, if there are not, the place is not truly public. Or urban.

The big problem is the street. Internal spaces with shops can dilute the attractions of the street outside, and the more successful they are, the greater the problem. How many more indoor spaces it might take to tip the scale is difficult to determine, but it is a matter the planning commissions should think very hard about. More immediate is the question of the internal space's relation to the street. If the space is underwritten by incentive zoning, it should not merely provide access to the public, it should invite it.

A good internal space should not be blocked off by bland walls. It should be visible from the street; the street and its surroundings should be highly visible from it; and between the two, physically

Place Ville Marie sequence shows how heavier flows can make for less congestion in doorways. People tend to queue up behind open doors; when there are so many people that all doors are open, everyone moves faster.

and psychologically, the connections should be easy and inviting. The Crystal Court of the IDS Building is a splendid example. It is transparent. You are in the center of Minneapolis, no mistake. You see it. There is the street and the neighboring buildings, and what most catches the eye are the flows of people through doorways and walkways. It is an easy place to get in and out of.

Most places are not. Typically, building entrances are overengineered affairs centered around a set of so-called revolving doors. The doors do not of themselves revolve; you revolve them. From a standing start, this requires considerable foot-pounds of energy. As does opening the swinging doors at the sides—which you are not supposed to use anyway. These doors are for emergency use. So there is frequently a sign saying PLEASE USE RE-VOLVING DOOR mounted on a pedestal blocking the center of the emergency door. Sometimes, for good measure, there is a second set of doors 15 or 20 feet inside the first.

All this is necessary, engineers say, for climate control and for an air seal to prevent stack-effect drafts in the elevator shafts. Maybe so. But on occasion revolving doors are folded to an open position. If you watch the entrances then, you will notice that the building still stands and no great drafts ensue. Watch the entrances long enough, and there is something else you will notice. The one time they function well is when they are very crowded.

I first noticed this phenomenon at Place Ville Marie in Montreal. I was clocking the flow through the main concourse entrance, a set of eight swinging doors. At 8:45 A.M., when the flow was 6,000 people an hour, there was a good bit of congestion, with many people lined up one behind another. Ten minutes later the flow was up to a peak rate of 8,000 people an hour (outside Tokyo, the heaviest I've ever clocked). Oddly, there was little congestion. People were moving faster and more easily, with little queuing.

The reason lies in the impulse for the open door. Some people are natural door openers. Most are not. Where there is a choice, they will follow someone who is opening a door. Sometimes they will queue up two or three deep rather than open a door themselves. Even where there are many doors, most of the time the bulk of the traffic will be self-channeled through one or two of them. As the crowd swells, however, an additional door will be opened, then another. The pace quickens. The headway between people shortens. In transportation planning, it is axiomatic that there should be a comfortable headway between people. In doorway situations, the opposite is true. If the interval between people shortens to 1.2 seconds or less, the doors don't get a chance to close. All or most of the doors will be open, and, instead of bunching at one or two of them, people will distribute themselves through the whole entrance.

One way to provide a good entrance, then, is to have big enough crowds. But there is another possibility. Why not leave a door open?

This novel approach has been followed for the entrance of an indoor park. As part of the new Philip Morris building, architect Ulrich Franzen has designed an attractive space that the Whitney Museum will operate as a kind of sculpture garden. An entrance that invited people in was felt to be very important. Before the energy shortage an air door would have been the answer, and had been so specified in the zoning code for covered pedestrian areas. But this was out of the question now. So, at the other end of the scale, was the usual revolving-door barricade.

To check the potentials of an open door, I did a simple study of heavily used entrances. I filmed rush-hour flows with a digital stop watch recorded on the film, and then calculated how many people used which parts of the entrance. Happily, the weather was mild, and at several of the entrances one or two doors would be wedged open. As at Place Ville Marie, it was to the open door that most people went. This does not mean that the other doors were redundant; even if one doesn't choose to use them, having the choice to do so lessens one's sense of crowding. But for sheer efficiency, it became clear, a small space kept open is better than a wider space that is closed. At the main concourse entry to the RCA building, two open doors at one side of an eight-door entrance accounted for two thirds of the people passing through during the morning rush hour. At Grand Central Station, most of those using the nine-door entrance at 42nd Street traversed open doors, and at any given time three doors accounted for the bulk of the traffic. The doors at Grand Central are old, in disrepair, and the glass is rarely cleaned. But they do work well.

Franzen's design for the entrance to the Philip Morris indoor park incorporates these simple findings. Visually, the entrance will be a stretch of glass 20 feet wide. At the center it will have a pair of automatic sliding doors. In good weather and at peak-use times, the doors will be kept open to provide a clear, six-foot entry. This should be enough for the likely peak flows. For overflows, and people who like to open doors, there will be an option of swinging doors at either side. In bad weather, the sliding doors will open automatically when people approach. In effect, there will be an ever-open door. It is to be hoped there will be many more.

Concourses and Megastructures
9

Unfortunately, more and more entrances to downtown complexes aren't doorways; they're escalators to underground places or to upper-level walkways. Putting spaces away from street level is one thing. Now planners are taking the street itself away from street level. In some cases the slope of a site calls for the extra levels. But in most cases the architectural acrobatics are being pursued as an end in themselves.

Why? Cities that have inferiority complexes want bold statements. Smaller cities seem particularly vulnerable. In those with conventional downtowns in trouble, officials are tempted to go whole hog in the other direction. So they set off on a pilgrimage to Montreal or Minneapolis and

bring back plans for upper-level walkway systems and for underground squares and concourses. What they do not often bring back, or much consider, is the context that makes these approaches work in the places where they work.

Minneapolis walkways, for example, work well in Minneapolis. There are good reasons. The walkways feed into the central place of the city, linking the main department stores and office buildings; they carry very heavy pedestrian flows, and in winter the flows are further increased by the fierce climate on the streets outside. High density is the crux. As the walkways extend outward from the center, the flows

fall off; so does the amount of retail business.

If a second level of stores is put up, what happens to the level below? A downtown of a given size can support just so many stores, and if a second level greatly increases the space available for them, something has to give. True, a new facility may pull enough additional patronage into the city to sustain the old as well as the new. But it may not. If that is the case, either the stores on the upper level will suffer, or the stores on the street, or, quite likely, both.

The other direction is underground. As a means of getting quickly and easily from

Left: Concourses can be pleasant places and Place Ville Marie is an example. Note the two men in a 100-percent conversation, always a good indication.
Below: There's not much up top at the Brunswick plaza in Chicago. Everything is down below.

the subway or train, underground concourses have long been useful. The potential that planners see is much more embracing. Increasingly, they look at underground places as environments in their own right—alternatives to the street for shopping, eating, and socializing. There is a strong emphasis on system. On maps of underground projects, bold lines and dotted lines link together in a comprehensive network which, on completion, will allow people to go from any one spot in the central business district to any other, enabling them to satisfy most of their downtown needs underground.

If planners had to spend more time in these places, they might have second thoughts about them. As environments, subterranean corridors are, for one thing, disorienting. If you stay awhile in one spot, you will be struck by the number of people appearing lost and coming up to ask directions. It is not for want of graphics. Helvetica-style type is laid on with abandon; there are directional signs everywhere, along with YOU ARE HERE illuminated maps. It is still easy to get lost, however. Part of the trouble is that underground systems are usually laid out symmetrically: North Corridor A is likely to be a mirror image of South Corridor B. Nothing is askew as it is up on the street; there's no landmark on which to get one's bearings, no sun to give a clue to east or west.

The places are drafty, especially near entrances. There are, furthermore, many abrupt variations in temperatures from one section to another. There are not the extremes one expects outdoors, but that is itself a problem; in-between climate poses more hazards than the strong, but known, climate up above. What kind of clothes should you wear? During a good part of the year, it is too warm for an overcoat, or too cool for regular clothing.

As shopping environments, concourses are fine for convenience items—newspapers, shoeshines, Xerox copies, automated bank branches. They are not right for the top of the line. There is something second class about basements, and that is the impression most of them convey. The schlock quotient is strong. Most concourses have an inordinate number of gift and card shops, pinball and electronic game galleries, and junk-food counters. The few that do have quality shops are usually part of a large complex in which the street level has been ruled out for retailing. This produces a captive clientele—which, of course, can be pointed to as proof that people like it underground.

The advantage of this kind of system lies largely in looking at maps of it. They seem so complete. But the completeness is not relevant to most pedestrians, nor perceived by them. If you check how the system is used, you will find that the great bulk of traffic is concentrated on the main connectors. Some people may find pleasure in being able to go from point A to D, then on to Z. But part of that pleasure lies in knowing that few other people know. As you poke out to the further reaches, the number of people you see drops markedly. So do benefit-cost ratios. Per foot, it costs just about as much to build the little-used segments as the main ones and as much to operate them.

Montreal's Place Ville Marie is underground, to be sure, and it works very well in Montreal. But there are other factors at work than undergroundness. As with the IDS center, Place Ville Marie is in the very center of the city, directly between the railroad station and the main shopping street. Because of the sharp slope of the site, one side is at street level. Daylight has been brought into the complex through four small courtyards with stairs to a large plaza above. And, as in Minneapolis, the winter climate is fierce (the day I took the pictures of the doorway it was minus 18 degrees—a temperature, it should be noted, that didn't keep good-size crowds

The Bonaventure Complex, Los Angeles.

off Ste. Catherine Street, the main shopping street). Once again, it is the context that makes the Montreal approach work.

Megastructures

The ultimate development in the flight from the street is the urban fortress. In the form of megastructures more and more of these things are being put up—huge, multipurpose complexes combining offices, hotels, and shops—such as Detroit's Renaissance Center, Atlanta's Omni International. Their distinguishing characteristic is self-containment. While they are supposed to be the salvation of downtown, they are often some distance from the center of downtown, and in any

event tend to be quite independent of their surroundings, which are most usually parking lots. The megastructures are wholly internalized environments, with their own life-support systems. Their enclosing walls are blank, windowless, and to the street they turn an almost solid face of concrete or brick.

A car is the favored means of entry. At Houston Center you can drive in from the freeway to the Center's parking garage, walk through a skyway to one tower, thence to another, work the day through, and then head back to the garage and the freeway without ever once having to set foot in Houston at all.

There wouldn't be much reason to. Down at the street level of Houston Center there are no store windows. There are no stores. There are not many people. The sole retail activity is a drive-in bank and the only acknowledgment that is

Above: Street side of the berm bordering the entrance of Renaissance Center in Detroit.
Left: The direct antithesis of the megastructure approach is Faneuil Hall marketplace in Boston. A large part of the activity takes place in the street, welcomed as an integral part of the complex.
Below: Houston Center looks like a fortress and is built like a fortress.

made of the pedestrian consists of flashing lights and signs telling him he'd better damn well watch out for cars.

The resemblance to fortresses is not accidental. It is the philosophic base. "Yes, they do look a little forbidding," says one proponent, "but they really have to. The fact is the only way we can lure middle-class shoppers back to downtown is to promise them security." So, in spirit as well as form, the interstate shopping mall is transplanted to downtown and security raised to the nth degree. The complexes abound with guards and elaborate electronic surveillance systems. Any kind of suspicious activity is quickly spotted and attended to (including, as I have found, the taking of photographs). Ports of entry from the city outside are few in number and their design is manifestly defensive. Where Renaissance Center faces Detroit there is a large concrete berm athwart the

Spiked ledge of Peachtree Plaza Hotel.

entrance. All that is lacking is a portcullis. But the message is clear. Afraid of Detroit? Come in and be safe.

The complexes bid to become larger. Increasingly, the megastructures are being combined with convention and sports facilities. Like megastructures, these tend to be located at the edge of downtown or beyond, and can be mated with megastructures via skybridges and concourses to form an almost completely closed circuit. As a result, some American cities now have two cities—regular city and visitor city.

Conventioneers sometimes complain of a lack of variety. A logical next step will be the creation within the complexes of fac-

similes of streets. There is one at Disneyland, and it is very popular; there are several at the White Flint Mall outside Washington, D.C. With similar showmanship, indoor theme parks could be set up to give an experience of the city without the dangers of it. In addition to such physical features as sidewalks and gas lights, barber poles, cigar-store Indians, and the like, street-like activities could be programmed, with costumed players acting as street people.

Another approach would be to tie in with real streets in the first place. There are some solid attractions in megastructures—excellent hotels and restaurants, good shops, waterfalls, elevators in glass pods, and public spaces of a drama and luxury not seen since the movie palaces of the twenties. Must isolation be a condition of their attraction? The megastructure thesis is somewhat self-proving. If people go in, it is argued, this proves they are seeking escape from the city and its insecurities. But does it? Do people go into Peachtree Plaza Center because there are spikes on its front ledge on Peachtree Street? They went in when there weren't spikes. Do people go into Renaissance Center because of the berm? Or despite it? The evidence suggests that they go in because there are attractions to enjoy. These attractions do not require separation from the city to be enjoyed, and are more enjoyable when not separated. Faneuil Hall Marketplace is witness to this. It's a bit hoked up, too, most shrewdly so, but it's part of a real city and it has a splendid sense of place.

This is what megastructures so lack. One feels somewhat disembodied in these places. Is it night? Or day? Spring? Or winter? And where are you? You cannot see out of the place. You do not know what city you are in, or if you are in a city at all. The complex could be at an airport or a new town. It could be in the East or the West. The piped music gives no cue.

Peachtree Street view of Peachtree Plaza.

It is the same as it is everywhere. You could be in a foreign country or on a space satellite. You are in a universal controlled environment.

And it is going to date very badly. Forms of transportation and their attendant cultures have historically produced their most elaborate manifestations just after they have entered the period of their obsolescence. So it may be with megastructures and the freeway era that bred them. They are the last convulsive embodiment of a time passing, and they are a wretched model for the future of the city.

89

Smaller Cities and Places
10

Will the factors that make a plaza or small space successful in one city work in another? Generally, the answer is yes—with one key variable to watch. It is scale, and it is particularly important for smaller cities. For a number of reasons, it is tougher for them to create lively spaces than it is for a big city.

Big cities have lots of people in their downtowns. This density poses problems, but it provides a strong supply of potential users for open spaces in most parts of the central business district. Where 3,000 people an hour pass by a site, a lot of mistakes can be made in design and a place may still end up being well used.

Smaller cities are not as compressed. True, some are blessed with a tight, well-defined center, with some fine old buildings to anchor it. But many others have loosened up; they have torn down old buildings and not replaced them, leaving much of the space open. Parking lots and garages become the dominant land use, often accounting for more than 50 percent of downtown. This is true also of some big cities—Houston, for one. Houston has some fine elements in its downtown, but they are so interspersed with parking lots that they don't connect very well with one another.

Many cities have diffused their downtowns by locating new "downtown" developments outside of downtown, or just far enough away that one element does not support the other. The distances need not

The recycling of the Reed Opera House in Salem, Oregon, into a complex of shops and restaurants reinforces the sense of place of the city.

be great. If you have to get into a car and drive, a place six blocks away might as well be a mile or more. That is precisely the kind of trouble you have in a number of cities. Kansas City's Crown Center, for example, is only 11 blocks from the central business district, but the two centers still remain more or less unconnected.

Cities in the 100,000–200,000 range are not just scaled-down versions of bigger cities. Relatively speaking, the downtowns of these smaller cities cover more space than the downtowns of bigger cities. Often their streets are wider, and their pedestrian densities much lower, with fewer people in any given area of the central business district. Sidewalk counts are a good index. If the number of passersby is under a rate of 1,000 per hour around noontime, a city could pave the street with gold for all the difference it would make. Something fundamental is missing: people. More stores, more offices, more reasons for being are what the downtown must have.

Some cities have sought to revitalize their downtowns by banning cars from the main street and turning it into a pedestrian mall. Some of these malls have worked well. Some have not. Again, the problem is diffusion. The malls may be too big for the number of people and the

amount of activities. This seems to be particularly the case with the smaller cities—which tend to have the largest malls.

What such cities need to do is to compress, to concentrate. Many of them were very low density to begin with; in some, most of the buildings are only two or three stories high. Spread over many downtown blocks are activities and people that might have come together in a critical mass had they been compressed into two or three. Such places are sad to see. So

many hopes, so many good intentions, so many fountains and play sculptures have gone into them. Yet they are nearly empty.

Smaller cities are also highly vulnerable to the competition of suburban shopping centers—in particular, the huge centralized ones going up next to interchanges. The suburban centers that do well are more urban in their use of space than the cities they are beating out. True, they are surrounded by a vast acreage of parking space, much of which is never used save

It's vogue in many small cities to have a second street level. But this tends to diffuse street activity. The most successful streets direct several floors of activity to one street level, as in Salem (*facing page*). So with New York's Madison Avenue (*left*). Its second storyness is an inherent part of its vitality.

on peak days. Unlike the earlier generation of linear shopping centers, however, the new ones are highly concentrated, one-stop places. You don't have to drive here for this and there for that. You enter an enclosed pedestrian system that is, in effect, a gigantic customer-processing machine.

A model for downtown? Some cities now think so. To beat suburbia at its own game, they have been inviting developers to put up shopping centers in downtown. The developers have responded with copies of their suburban models, with very little adaptation: concrete boxes, geared to people who drive to them, that have little relationship to the sidewalks or surrounding buildings of the city. These mini-megastructures may be an efficient setting for merchandising of the middle range; in suburbia, they provide something of a social center as well. But they are not for the downtown. They are the antithesis of what downtown should be.

Cities do best when they intensify their unique strengths. Salem, Oregon, for example, at one time thought its last, best hope would be a suburban-type shopping complex, complete with a skyway or two

for razzle-dazzle. But somehow it didn't seem like Salem. The city decided on an opposite approach. It is filling in empty spaces with buildings to the scale of the place, putting glass canopies over sidewalks, converting alleys into shopping ways, tying strong points with pedestrian spaces and sitting areas. An old opera house has been converted into a complex of stores with felicitous results, and other old structures may be recycled, too. In sum, Salem has embarked on a plan that works with the grain of the city.

It is significant that the cities doing best by their downtowns are the ones doing best at historic preservation and reuse. Fine old buildings are worthwhile in their own right, but there is a greater benefit involved. They provide discipline. Architects and planners like a blank slate. They usually do their best work, however, when they don't have one. When they have to work with impossible lot lines and bits and pieces of space, beloved old eyesores, irrational street layouts, and other such constraints, they frequently produce the best of their new designs—and the most neighborly.

Triangulation

11

We have gone over the principal factors that make a place work. But there is one more factor. I call it triangulation. By this I mean that process by which some external stimulus provides a linkage between people and prompts strangers to talk to each other as though they were not. There are, say, two men standing at a street corner. A third man appears. He hoists a sign and begins a loud harangue on the single tax. This links the two men. Casually, they exchange comments on the human comedy before them, in a tone of voice usually reserved for close friends.

Street characters make a city more amicable. Mr. Magoo, who volunteers as a traffic director in midtown New York, will always draw a crowd, and his performance will draw its members together. The person standing next to you is likely to tell you all about his history, or ask you who in the world he is. The Witch, a raunchy woman who jeers at the dignified and spits at little children, is quite deplorable. Strangers exchange shocked glances. But they smile, too, as if they were on her side.

The stimulus can be a physical object or sight. At the small park at the Promenade in Brooklyn Heights there is a spectacular view of the towers of lower Manhattan across the East River. It is a great conversation opener and strangers normally remark each other on it. When you come upon such a scene, it would be rude not to.

A street band draws people. So does sculpture, particularly the kind that people like to touch, such as Dubuffet's stainless-steel "Rag Lady" (*above*) and "Four Trees" (*left*).

95

Sculpture can have strong social effects. Before and after studies of the Chase Manhattan plaza showed that the installation of Dubuffet's "Four Trees" has had a beneficent impact on pedestrian activity. People are drawn to the sculpture, and drawn through it: they stand under it, beside it; they touch it; they talk about it. At the Federal Plaza in Chicago, Alexander Calder's huge stabile has had similar effects.

Musicians and entertainers draw people together. Rockefeller Plaza and the First National Bank of Chicago regularly schedule touring school bands, rock groups, and the like. As noted in the discussion of the amphitheater effect, however, the real show is usually the audience. Many people will be looking as much at each other as at what's on the stage.

It is not the excellence of the act that is important. It is the fact that it is there that bonds people, and sometimes a really bad act will work even better than a good one. Street entertainers, for example, can be very, very bad. One of the best of the bad is a young magician whose pattern is so corny and predictable that you are virtually forced into conversation with your neighbor. With each of the magician's asides, the onlookers get increasingly jovial, delivering more of their own asides,

and engaging in much banter and exchange of opinions. Also, the magician collects a nice sum.

But good performers are best. Among them are the mimes. In a typical sequence, a mime walks up to two junior-executive types and draws a huge square in the air. The crowd laughs, and the junior executives laugh. Cops are a great foil. As one of them moves across a plaza, a mime will walk behind him aping his gait. The cop turns around, laughs, and shakes the mime's hand. The crowd laughs and whistles its approval.

The most adroit routine is that of a young acrobat. As he is collecting money from the crowd, he tries to spot a policeman. If one is standing nearby, enjoying himself, the acrobat suddenly recoils and in a loud voice begs the cop not to hit him again. The crowd, furious at police brutality, gives more money.

A virtue of street acts is their unexpectedness. When people form a crowd around an entertainer—it happens very quickly, in 40 or 50 seconds—they look much like children who have come upon a treat; some will be smiling in simple delight. These moments are true recreation, though rarely thought of as such, certainly not by the retailers who try so hard to outlaw them. But there is something of great value here, and it should be fostered.

Why not invite entertainers onto a plaza instead of banning them? One corporation is considering a plan to welcome the best of the street entertainers to its new building. The entertainers would be given the equivalent of several good collections to do their act.

Most of the elements that have the triangulation effect are worthwhile in their own right. Simply on aesthetic grounds, Dubuffet's "Four Trees" much improves the scale and sense of place in the Chase

The best show window on Lexington Avenue looks into the sanctuary of St. Peter's Church. Passersby stop to look and comment: "Wow!" "That's not my idea of a church!" "Isn't it gorgeous!"

In Praise of Odds and Ends

As I conclude, let me say a word about large spaces. The emphasis in this manual has been on small spaces. But this is not to scant the desirability of large ones. The question is sometimes raised whether it is better to have a Central Park or an equivalent amount of space in small parks. There is no comparability. Central Park is a magnificent space on a large scale, and it does something for New York that no aggregation of small spaces could. Thanks to the genius of Frederick Law Olmsted, it should be added, Central Park is also a host of small spaces, and people experience it as such.

The fact is, however, that for the foreseeable future the opportunities in the center city are going to be for small spaces. And there are great opportunities. True, costs are prodigious—even in the case of incentive zoning, expensive trade-offs are included. But the costs are high because so many people are to be served. A less costly place somewhere else can be a poor bargain.

Manhattan plaza. But the social effects are important. By observing them, we can find how they can be anticipated and planned.

I am not, heaven forfend, going on to argue for places of maximum gregariousness, social directors for plazas. Anomie would be preferable. What I'm suggesting, simply, is that we make places friendlier. We know how. In both the design and management of spaces, there are many ways to make it much easier for people to mingle and meet. It would be no bad idea to move more in this direction.

Above: A temporary art gallery.
Below: One of the best spots in New York is a ledge at 57th Street and Madison Avenue. It usually has sun and is protected from the wind.

Some of the most felicitous spaces, furthermore, are leftovers, niches, odds and ends of space that by happy accident work very well for people. At 57th Street and Madison Avenue in New York there is a bank with two window ledges. They're low enough for sitting and are recessed enough to provide wind protection. There is sun all day, a parade of passersby, and at the corner a vendor squeezing fresh orange juice. It is a splendid urban place. There are other such places, most provided by inadvertence. Think what might be provided if someone planned it.

Bus stops are often amiable places and more could be. Observe the people there

and you will find that many are not waiting for the bus. They just like the activity. Usually the only amenities are a bench or two and a sign with the bus routes. If overhead shelter were provided and a bit more space, these places could be far more amenable. And why not bus-stop parklets? In Billings, Montana, they are fashioning a small one with groupings of benches and with trees overhead. It is likely to become the city's best meeting place.

The furniture of the street can make places work better but, again, customarily it's more by inadvertence than design. Trash receptacles are an example. New York City provided millions of dollars worth of heavy concrete objects with flat tops. As receptacles, they were terrible, the tops acting as trash dispensers. But they were excellent for some other purposes. People used them as small tables, sometimes sat on them, used them as ledges for re-sorting packages.

There would seem to be a lesson here. So with fire hydrants and standpipes. Both are useful for tying shoelaces, and the standpipes are good for sitting as well. And why not shelves? Just as an experiment it would be interesting to see what would happen if buildings provided an extra ledge about four to five feet high. The Japanese are more inventive than we at such matters. On the sidewalks at the entrances to some department stores, ledges are provided for sitting, for placing things: there are ashtrays, benches, phone booths. There's not much space, but it is very heavily and well used.

We do not have much sidewalk space either, but we are going to have more. We have given a disproportionate amount of our street space to vehicles, and the time has come to start giving some of it back to the pedestrians from whom it was taken. To meet federal air-quality standards, some cities may have to eliminate parking on downtown streets. This can free up

one or two lanes of space. Rather than have the space revert to traffic—and thus induce more of it—the space should be given back to the sidewalks. If it is, there will be enough room for many kinds of pedestrian amenities—such as bus-stop parklets, sitting places, and sidewalk cafes.

I am, in sum, bespeaking busy places. Too busy? Too crowded? I think not. As we have seen, people have a nice sense of the number that is right for a place, and it is they who determine how many is too many. They do not, furthermore, seek to get away from it all. If they did, they would go to the lonely empty places where there are few people. But they do not. They go to the lively places where there are many people. And they go there by choice—not to escape the city, but to partake of it.

It is wonderfully encouraging that places people like best of all, find least crowded, and most restful are small spaces marked by a high density of people and a very efficient use of space.

I end, then, in praise of small spaces. The multiplier effect is tremendous. It is not just the number of people using them, but the larger number who pass by and enjoy them vicariously, or the even larger number who feel better about the city center for knowledge of them. For a city, such places are priceless, whatever the cost. They are built of a set of basics and they are right in front of our noses.

If we will look.

Appendix A:
Time-Lapse Filming

Above: A typical time-lapse setup with a digital clock. The clock will later prove very useful in the difficult job of evaluation, providing a place mark. *Facing page:* Cameras set up for regular, slow motion, and time-lapse study of a busy street corner.

If you were trying to conceive an ideal device for studying people's behavior in public places, you might come up with these specifications:

a small, inconspicuous camera that would:

cover any desired angle of view from wide angle to telephoto close-up;

automatically take a picture at any set interval from a half second to 10 minutes;

run unattended for up to 48 hours;

automatically adjust to any change in light from dawn to dusk and beyond;

record to the hundredth of a second the exact time each picture was taken.

With the growth of a mass market for Super-8 photography, a by-product has been just such a device—small, light, excellent, and inexpensive. With it you can multiply yourself as an observer, study many areas simultaneously, and do it with an accuracy and stamina few humans could match. You can store time, retrieve it for later study, replay it to others, in dramatic and compelling form.

You would expect this to spur a widespread use of time lapse—in schools, colleges, and universities, planning commissions, park and recreation agencies, transportation agencies, among shopping-mall and commercial developers. Not so.

There have been many starts, often quite enthusiastic, much dabbling, but remarkably few sustained efforts.*

I think I know why. In our research, we have gone through the cycle, done our floundering, made every mistake. But, thanks to the long time span of our study, we got our second wind and finally learned a few simple but important lessons. The crux is evaluation. Taking the

* For a fine exception see Gerald Davis and Virginia Ayers "Photographic Recording of Environmental Behavior," in W. Michelson, ed., *Behavioral Research Methods in Environmental Design* (Stroudsburg, Pa.: Dowden Hutchinson & Ross, 1975). They have used photography extensively for environmental analysis, and their experience with time-lapse methods and equipment parallels ours in key respects—in particular, the importance of evaluation and of precision in time coding the film. We use an external clock; they have a camera modified to record the time directly on each frame.

film is easy. So is showing it. It's even fun. But when you start figuring out, frame by frame, what the film has to tell, and what it means, you will find the process can be enormously time consuming, and, before long, tedious. That's where it all breaks down. Unless you master this phase, you will not stay the course.

Happily, there are ways to shortcut the tedium, greatly speed up evaluation, and in the process make it more accurate. It won't be fun, as I will note, but there are many tales in all those little pictures and the finding of them can be rewarding.

Equipment

First a look at the basic equipment. We used a battery of Braun Nizo S-56 Super-8 cameras. These are marvels of compression and contain a built-in intervalometer

with a range from six frames a second to one frame every 10 minutes. They have a fine Schneider Zoom Lens from 7mm wide-angle setting to 56mm. These particular cameras are fairly expensive. The latest model, S-560, lists for about $500 and can be obtained for about $300 at discount. But less-expensive cameras with intervalometers have been coming onto the market. One that works well is the Minolta XL 401, selling at a discount price of about $170. It is very small and light, with a built-in intervalometer and an f 1.2 lens. The zoom range is limited, 8.5mm to 34mm, but it is the wide-angle setting you will use most of the time, and it can be widened further with a supplementary lens—such as the Curvatar, available from Spiratone in New York for about $40.

Camera Placement

Setting up the camera is a task that should be easy but is not. First you have to find a good perch. Ideally, it should provide a clear view of the pedestrian area from a low, oblique angle. For a street corner, for example, this means a second- or third-story perch on the other side of the street, most likely an office. Although the perch should be secure enough that you can leave the camera there unattended, it's not good to have people working nearby in the same room. At first they are interested in the project and friendly. That steady click gets them after a while, however, and your welcome can wear pretty quickly.

There should be enough space behind the window so that the camera can be set back and not be easily visible from the street. Since you may have reflection problems, you should be able to open the window. If not, it should be clear and clean. Few are. One of our biggest technical challenges has been finding ways to clean the outside of immovable windows.

Sometimes you will find that your best perch for a particular area is a rooftop or a terrace. It is vital that you secure the camera with a chain or wire. There is a very real hazard that the camera will fall or be blown over and land in the street with serious consequences. I had to pay a very stiff premium for liability insurance to cover our group. But when I think of the possible hazards involved, I do not think the premium was so bad.

More often than not one part of the area that you are studying will be obscured by the edge of a building or a sign. Don't fret. Study, on the ground, the normal use of the obscure area in relation to the rest of it. These relationships are usually fairly constant, and observation of a large part will give you a fairly accurate measure of the whole.

Clock Placement

You will want a clock in the picture. It's not so much to tell the time. It's to mark your place. When later you begin evaluating the film you will find yourself going backwards and forwards, tracking this action and that, and you will easily lose your place. Are the three men in black the same three that blocked the doorway? Or is this a different bunch? It is amazing how many incidents take place just like the ones before them and how easily you can get mixed up as to who, precisely, is on first. A number for each picture of the sequence is invaluable. This is what a clock gives you.

The placement of the clock is important. It should be visible in the lower part of the picture frame, and it should show the time to the second. Originally we used an over-sized alarm clock with a sweep-second hand. We now use a digital clock with an LED display of six digits, excellent for night work. It requires a 110-volt outlet, but before long there should be battery-powered models available.

The trick is to position the clock so that it is close enough to the camera to be clearly legible, yet just far enough away to be in focus with the rest of the scene.

With a lens set at wide angle, the depth of field is great enough that a clock placed about three feet away from the camera will be in focus when the background is in focus. Only when the light is very low and the automatic diaphragm is wide open will the clock be somewhat out of focus. Be sure to have a depth-of-field chart handy so that you will know what the hyperfocal distance is—in effect, the setting that best straddles background and foreground.

Lens Setting

How wide should the angle be? In most cases, the wider the better. If you narrow the angle to a telephoto setting, you will get more close-up detail. But, usually, you do not need the detail. What you need is the context of the scene—the wings, so to speak, of your stage. If you are studying a street corner, for example, you should include at least 30 feet of the sidewalk on either side. Where people come from, where they go to, can be quite important.

We found this crucial in a study on loitering we did in cooperation with the police. They asked us to study the entrance to a bar that was the main rendezvous for drug dealers on 42nd Street. The police wanted to find out what effects, if any, periodic police sweeps would have on the dealers' activity. The dealers were quite brazen and day and night would stand conspicuously in front of the bar. But there was some satellite activity extending some 40 feet on either side and, to understand what was going on in front of the bar, you had to understand what was going on there. When the police walked conspicuously by or stood near the bar, the dealers moved away, but not always very far. In this case, we used two cameras, one for extreme wide-angle use, another set in a normal focus length to give more detailed coverage of the bar itself. (Incidentally, we found that when the po-lice moved away from the bar, it took all of 30 to 50 seconds before the dealers reappeared.)

Interval

All things being equal, the longer the interval between frames the better. For one thing, the camera will operate longer before a refill is necessary. As a rule of thumb, you can calculate that the number of seconds in the interval is the number of hours the film will last. For recording sitting patterns in plazas, we used 10-second intervals. This allowed us to set up the camera at 8:00 in the morning and let it run until 6:00 in the evening. It was also a useful interval for evaluation. You can simply multiply each frame by 10 seconds to figure the elapsed time.

The interval must be short enough, however, so that you will not miss any significant movement. For sitting patterns, 10 seconds is fine, but if you are studying pedestrian movements at a street crossing, you want a much shorter interval. Two seconds is about right. If the interval were much longer, someone could walk through the field of view between clicks.

In such situations it is often a good idea to set up two cameras: one for the widest-possible angle and a long interval, another to give a closer view at a much shorter interval. It does not take much more effort to set up two cameras than one.

You should record intervals and other data on each roll of film. One way is to write in large block letters on a sheet of paper the place, date, time, interval, and focus setting: hold it about three feet in front of the camera and film it for about three seconds. For good measure you should write the same data, this time in very small letters, on the return address label before you send the film cartridge off for processing. Don't forget to do this. If you're shooting a lot of film, you will find your unaided memory a poor substitute.

Film Stock

Regular Kodachrome is superb. It has a very high resolution, high contrast and vivid colors. It also has a very tough emulsion, no small advantage considering the wear and tear it will later get. The resolution is so high that for all practical purposes Super 8 yields an image quite satisfactory for analysis. I have a complete 16mm time-lapse setup, and very expensive and cumbersome it is. But it is an advantage only in special circumstances, such as a need for optical imposition.

Kodachrome is made to be projected, and if you are showing the camera original on a small screen, it will look just as good as a print of a 16mm film would. On one TV program I showed both original Super 8 and 16mm prints. There was no noticeable difference in quality between them.

Super 8's small size does have a drawback. Any dirt or marks on the film are hugely magnified. This is especially the case with the dirt and bits of emulsion that build up on the edges of the aperture plate in the camera. They're easy to overlook, but they leave a permanent memento, with every frame marked with a bunch of stalactites at the top. Be sure and clean the plate frequently with a cotton swab dipped in alcohol.

Super-8 has another drawback. It's hard to get a decent print from it. Kodachrome's high contrast becomes more contrasty in duplication, and the result is most disappointing. Other stocks yield somewhat better prints, but as of this writing the state of the art is not good. For documentary film intended for wide showing in medium or large auditoriums, 16mm is a necessity.

Viewers and Projectors

For evaluation, your chief tool will be the viewer. Viewers have a rotating prism mechanism, and the emulsion does not touch a hard surface. You can run the film back and forth without hurting it. The disadvantage of the rotating prism is a not-very-sharp image. Try to get the best-quality viewer you can afford. The extra money will be worth it.

Projectors can be used for evaluation. I have a Kodak Ektagraphic that can run the frames at different speeds, advance the film a frame at a time, and so on. It is a very expensive piece of equipment, very heavy, and like virtually all projectors it can rough up film. It is excellent for analyzing film before a group. But for regular analysis a viewer is better.

For showing a film, a small, lightweight projector with variable speed control will be quite satisfactory. There are several good models available in the $100-$150 range. For single-frame capability you will have to pay more, but this is not necessary. Whatever the model, a tremendous trifle is a clean film gate. As with cameras, you should develop an obsessive regard for frequent cleaning. One gob of dirt will draw a line through the whole reel, and the next and the next, and if it's original footage you're showing, the damage is serious.

No matter how clean the projector, it will rough up the film. You have something of a dilemma. A print will safeguard your original, but the original will look much better. You will probably yield to temptation and run the original. A partial solution is to have the original coated. One process just developed, Photogard, by Minnesota Mining and Manufacturing, can coat the film with a protective layer impervious to scratches. It is available now for 16mm film at 3.5 cents a foot, but eventually may become available for Super-8. (For inquiries write Minnesota Mining and Manufacturing at 321 West 44th Street, New York, New York, 10036.)

You will find time-lapse film extremely useful for communicating the results of a study to interested groups. You can anticipate that initially there will be much laughter at the pictures of the funny people rushing back and forth. But the members of the audience will be quite impressed and they will feel personally involved. Here, in highly condensed form, are primary facts of their own area, and they can draw conclusions themselves. They do, and that is why the conclusions are so persuasive to them.

The process is particularly important with merchants. Some have a surprisingly inaccurate idea of the pedestrian life around them, and in almost all downtown improvement programs one or more merchants will be fearful that the amenities will draw undesirables. In one such case, we made a continuous film record of several days of sitting on some test benches. The benches proved an immediate success, were particularly well used by older people, and not once did anyone lie down on them, undesirable or otherwise. The merchants saw and were convinced.

Night Work

The combination of a very fast lens, as in the Minolta XL, and Kodak's High-Speed Ektachrome can give excellent nighttime coverage. In the police study I mentioned, for the main illumination there was a street light in the front of the bar. As things happened, the street light went out the night we started and stayed out for the next three nights. The only light was the reflected light from the bar itself. It proved quite enough. Some of the film we "pushed"—that is, overdeveloped to compensate for the low light—and it looked quite overexposed.

Slow Motion

Occasionally we use slow motion. At 48 to 64 frames a second, you consume a lot of film very quickly; for sustained analysis, it is just too expensive. But there is another possibility: retroactive slow motion. If there is a sequence in your film that you would like to analyze in detail, you can have an optical print of it made with each successive frame repeated four times. The result does not have the smooth flow of true slow motion; it is somewhat jerky, like an instant replay on television. But it is an excellent expository device.

The case of Fast Brown and Slow Blue is an example. In the course of examining hundreds of feet of film of pedestrian crossing patterns, we came across a fine example of pedestrian skill. A man in a brown suit was striding imperiously across the corner. On a direct collision course, a man in a blue suit walked slowly toward him. At the critical moment, the man in blue lifted his left hand to his head; thrown off balance, the man in brown stopped, then detoured a few steps to his right before proceeding. It looked at regular speed just like two pedestrians. A freeze-frame analysis, however, shows how sophisticated and adroit such moves can be.

Street Filming

Some kinds of activities are best photographed not in time lapse or slow motion, but at normal speed: foot movements, behavior at doorways, pedestrian crossing patterns, and the like. I use 16mm for much of this kind of work. It is more expensive, but there are several advantages. One is the ability to superimpose a digital clock on the film via double exposure. In a completely dark room I photograph an illuminated digital clock, placed to appear in the lower right-hand corner of the film frame. I run off several rolls of film and then back-wind them. I thus have what might be called pre-clocked film stock, and, whatever phenomena I film with it, there will be a digital count on each frame. It won't be of the exact time, of course, but it will precisely indicate elapsed time.

The bulk of our research footage is of pedestrians in everyday situations—their meeting rituals, how they say goodbye, shmoozing patterns, and the like. As with time lapse, some of this footage is shot from a perch with both wide-angle and telephoto settings. Most, however, is shot at eye level with the camera hand held, as close as possible to the people being photographed.

Advice: move in closer. You want to be unobtrusive, yes, but the main point is to get good coverage and this usually means up close. If you're not, your subjects will be obscured by passersby, and you will miss the little nuances, movements, and facial expressions that can be so important.

The key to unobtrusiveness is misdirection. For a while, we experimented with right-angle mirror attachments. These are too tricky, and sometimes call attention to the deception. Through simpler techniques, we've found we can get surprisingly close and stay there without the subjects' being aware of it. Here is how.

Do not point the camera. Cradle it in your hands so that it is pointing sideways. With practice you will find that you can frame the scene rather accurately. We mount bubble levels on the tops of our cameras. When the bubble shows that the camera is tilted slightly upwards, you will have your subject fairly well centered. When the lens is set at its widest angle, it will give you considerable margin for error, and there are few focus problems.

Do not look directly at your subjects. More to the point, don't get caught doing it. If you meet their eyes, they will instantaneously recognize what you are up to. Your peripheral vision is good enough that you can appear to be looking elsewhere and still have a good idea of what's going on.

Super 8 has several advantages for this kind of photography. The cameras are quite small. They make very little noise, and you can pop in a new cartridge in a second. Perhaps most important, there are so many other people with Super 8 cameras that you appear to be just another tourist.

Even with 16mm, however, you can do close-in work. With a turret-model Beaulieu, for example, I use a 10mm wide-angle lens. There is a noise problem, but it is due not so much to the sound of the motor running as to the audible click when it stops. I try to mask this by moving away before ending the sequence or by setting the click to coincide with a loud street noise.

There is one group of people who will spot you no matter what your stratagem: children. They will drive you crazy with their questions. Hey, mister, what channel will this be on? Take my picture. They make funny faces in front of the lens. There is nothing for it but to indulge them with some preventive photography until, at length, they mug themselves out and leave you be.

Safety

Photography can be an invasion of privacy. This is a problem in documentary photography, and a good rule is not to show publicly people in embarrassing or compromising situations. For research footage, everything is a fair subject. But I try never to intrude on a situation that is truly private, or should be: a couple in an argument, a person crying in grief. Most day-in-day-out situations, however, are quite public and, happily, these are the most rewarding from a research point of view.

A bigger problem is safety. Some people object strenuously to being photographed: in particular, street vendors, three-card monte operators, and the like. They do not like to have their picture taken, and I have often been threatened. Then there are the cranks, some of whom mistakenly believe it is illegal to photograph on the street without their permission. The worst of the lot are people who are not being photographed, but who object to someone else's being photographed. In all such situations, the wise course is not to argue. Vanish.

The real danger comes in photographing illicit activities, especially when you do it without realizing it. Our narrowest call was when we set up a perch on the fourth floor of a building in the middle of a block on 101st Street. The object was to observe the social life on the stoops and fire escapes. Before long, Cadillacs with out-of-state licenses began stopping in front of the building opposite, and there was considerable movement in and out of the basement door. A wholesale heroin operation was under way. We thought it judicious to withdraw. On another occasion, we had our camera focused on the whore, pimp, and dope complex around a seedy old hotel. At length it was discerned that a look-out with binoculars was alerting people to the impending arrival of police cars. Then, one day, we saw on the film that the binoculars were trained directly on our camera. We withdrew.

Evaluation

Now comes the time when you sit down with the viewer and study the film frame by frame. This is the critical point in the whole process, and I am convinced that the main reason there has been so little systematic use of time lapse is the failure to master the tedium and ambiguities of this stage. To repeat, time lapse does not save time; it stores it.

When you get around to evaluation, you will find that some kinds of activity are relatively easy to evaluate. The study of street-corner conversations is a case in point. As you wind the film through the

viewer and watch the people moving this way and that, the people who *don't* move stand out very clearly. It is easy to note when they arrived on the scene and how long they stayed there. We plot the data on map overlays. To make a simple map, we put a sheet of acetate on the ground glass of the viewer and trace the scene.

Most activity is more difficult to evaluate. The problem is the same as it is with direct observation on the ground. There are so many bits of information in front of you as to be somewhat overwhelming, and, by looking at everything, you may see nothing. One reaction is to begin a slow, labored recording of a mass of data frame by frame. You will not last the course this way. It is dreadfully boring.

Speed and bravado are essential. What you have to do is to interrogate the film. Hypothesize; ask questions of the film— one question at a time, and run through the film quickly. Who's walking on the left instead of the right—mostly women? Or men? What happens when they walk three abreast? Are there any hour-to-hour changes in the rhythm of the flow? Many questions will lead to dead ends. But one or two will yield results.

Speed helps. As you run the film back and forth, you will see things you otherwise would not. This is the creative phase of evaluation. It is not the time to worry about accuracy. Time enough for that later.

Speed can help in another respect. Sometimes, you will want to run through the film at regular film speed of 18 or 24 frames per second. This vastly compresses time and movement and, as with slow motion, helps you see patterns more difficult to discern otherwise. We used this speeding-up technique in a study of traffic on Broadway and Seventh Avenue at Times Square. Was there space for a pedestrian strip? The film showed, in vivid yellow, that the two avenues were essentially taxi alleys; that most of the taxis traveled in only a few of the lanes, moved as fast as the lights would allow, and were most numerous when there was the least need for them.

Such reconnaissances tell you what threads to follow in detail. The next step is frame-by-frame analysis, and slow going it can be, for accuracy now becomes important. Relatively speaking, however, even here a measure of speed is in order. It is a little bit like playing a bridge hand. If you take too much time, you will forget your cards: you play your cards much better if you play them with dispatch. Was that car straddling the line in lane two or three? Did black suit belong to the group of three at the left or the two at the right? The scene is rife with ambiguities, and you must make arbitrary decisions and stick with them.

It is now that you will appreciate the importance of a clock in the picture. It gives you your reference points. If red hat enters plaza left at 2:20:07, you jot down the number on your worksheet, go on ahead to see what red hat will do, and then, finished with red hat, wind the film back to frame 2:20:07 and pick up the next person to track. It can still get you confused—frequent coffee breaks are vital—but having precise numbers for any action or juncture will vastly speed up your evaluation.

In preparing the chart on pages 70-71 on the day in the life at the ledge at Seagram, I spent over 100 man-hours in front of a viewer. I think that chart was worth the effort. But the time spent was simply too much for the technique to be reproducible. Since then, we have learned to cut the time by over half, and with no loss of accuracy. When we have cross-checked each other's annotation of particular sequences, the margin of difference is rarely more than 3 percent.

Let me emphasize again that you have to know what to look for or you will not see it. Direct observation is the prerequisite. If through direct observation you have gained a good idea of the usual routine at a place, you will see many more things in a time-lapse film of the place than you would otherwise. This also works backwards. After you have evaluated a film and put it away, you may spot a pattern that you had never previously noticed. This can prompt you to a fruitful reevaluation of the time-lapse film.

One day while going over a film of a blind beggar at work, I noticed that another blind beggar appeared on the scene and began rattling his cup some 40 feet in back of the first beggar. I was fascinated to find out how one affected the other's trade. The first beggar, while staying in the same spot, kept making a shuffling motion and moving his cup. The other remained stationary. The moving beggar received roughly three times as many contributions from passersby as the other. I went back over a number of films of beggars I had shot several years previously. Now I had a whole series of new questions to ask, and the films proved far more revealing than they had been before.

Finally, let me mention an occupational hazard not usually touched on in texts on research. When you study a place and chart it and map it, you begin to acquire a proprietary right in it. You do not reason this. Obviously, you have no such right. But you feel it. It is your place. You earned it.

You feel that way about people, too. As you find out more about their patterns of behavior and become able to predict them, you gain a sense of power, as though, by anticipating what they will do, you are yourself causing them to do it. When I walk down a street I have long studied, I am often enormously pleased to see what is going on, and I am pleased with myself as well. There are my people out there. They are acting as they should be acting. There are two women in a 100-percent conversation in just the right spot.

110

There is a shmoozer rocking up and down on his heel. There are two men exchanging goodbyes. Soon they will begin all over again. And they do. How satisfying!

Appendix B:
Digest of Open-Space Zoning
Provisions New York City

In 1961 New York City enacted a zoning resolution that gave developers a floor-area bonus for providing plaza space. For each square foot of plaza space, the builder was allowed 10 feet of additional commercial floor area. The requirement of the plazas was that they be accessible to the public at all times. That, as it turned out, was about all they were.

The 1975 amendments required that plazas be *amenable* to the public as well, and laid down specific guidelines for insuring that they would be. The guidelines are presented here in slightly abridged form, and are followed by comparable provisions enacted in 1977 for residential buildings.

1975 Zoning Amendments

Seating

There shall be a minimum of 1 linear foot of seating for each 30 square feet of urban plaza area, except that for urban plazas fronting upon a street having a grade change of at least 2.25 feet in 100 feet or for through-block urban plazas, there shall be a minimum of 1 linear foot of seating for each 40 square feet of urban plaza area.

Seating shall have a minimum depth of 16 inches. Seating with backs at least 12 inches high shall have a minimum depth of 14 inches. Seating 30 inches or more in depth shall count double provided there is access to both sides.

Seating higher than 36 inches and lower than 12 inches above the level of the adjacent walking surface shall not count toward meeting the seating requirements.

The tops of walls including but not limited to those which bound planting beds, fountains, and pools may be counted as seating when they conform to the dimensional standards above.

Movable seating or chairs, excluding seating of open air cafes, may be credited as 30 inches of linear seating per chair.

No more than 50 percent of the credited linear seating capacity may be in movable seats which may be stored between the hours of 7 P.M. and 7 A.M.

Steps, seats in outdoor amphitheaters, and seating of open air cafes do not count toward the seating requirements.

For the benefit of handicapped persons, a minimum of 5 percent of the required seating shall have backs.

Planting and Trees

At least one tree of 3.5 inches caliper or more shall be planted for each 25 feet of the entire street frontage of the zoning lot. They shall be planted with gratings flush to grade in at least 200 cubic feet of soil per tree, with a depth of soil at least 3 feet 6 inches.

Trees within an urban open space: For an urban plaza 1,500 square feet or more in area, 4 trees are required. For an urban plaza 5,000 square feet or more in area, 6 trees are required. For an urban plaza 12,000 square feet or more in area, 1 tree is required for every 2,000 square feet, or fraction thereof, of urban plaza area. Where trees are planted within an urban open space, they shall measure at least 3.5 inches in caliper at the time of planting. They shall be planted in at least 200 cubic feet of soil with a depth of soil of at least 3 feet 6 inches and be planted either with gratings flush to grade, or in a planting bed with a continuous area of at least 75

square feet exclusive of bounding wall, and at a maximum spacing of 25 feet apart.

Planting: When planting beds are provided, they shall have a soil depth of at least 2 feet for grass or other ground cover, and 3 feet for shrubs.

Retail Frontage

Except for that portion of a sidewalk widening along a narrow street, at least 50 percent of the total frontage of building walls of the development fronting on an urban open space, or fronting on an arcade adjoining an urban open space, exclusive of such frontage occupied by vertical circulation elements, building lobbies, and frontage used for subway access, shall be allocated for occupancy by retail or service establishments permitted by the applicable district regulations, but not including banks, loan offices, travel agencies, or airline offices. In addition, libraries, museums, and art galleries shall be permitted. All such uses shall be directly accessible from the urban open space or adjoining arcade.

Lighting

Urban open spaces shall be illuminated throughout with an overall minimum average level of illumination of not less than 2 horizontal foot candles (lumens per foot). Such level of illumination shall be maintained throughout the hours of darkness. Electrical power shall be supplied by 1 or more outlets furnishing a total of 1,200 watts of power for every 4,000 sq. ft., or fraction thereof, of an urban open space area, except for a sidewalk widening.

Circulation and Access

An urban plaza shall be open to use by the public at all times, with direct access from an adjoining public sidewalk or sidewalk widening along at least 50 percent of its total length of frontage. Along the remaining length of frontage, in order to allow maximum visibility from the street to the urban plaza, no wall may be constructed averaging higher than 36 inches above nor at any point higher than 5 feet above curb level of the nearest adjoining street.

The level of an urban plaza shall not at any point be more than 3 feet above nor 3 feet below the curb level of the nearest adjoining street.

Where there is a grade change of at least 2.25 feet in 100 along a portion of a street fronted upon for a distance of at least 75 feet by an urban plaza with an area of 10,000 square feet or more, the level of such urban plaza may be at any elevation which is not more than either 5 feet above or below curb level of the nearest adjoining street. Along the length of frontage not required for access, no wall higher than 36 inches above the level of the urban plaza may be constructed.

Where an entry to a subway station exists in the sidewalk area of a street on which an urban plaza fronts and such entry is not replaced within the urban plaza itself, the urban plaza shall be developed at the same elevation as the adjacent sidewalk for a distance of at least 15 feet in all directions from the entry superstructure. Such urban plaza area around a subway station entry shall be free of all obstructions.

Where an entry to a subway station is provided within the urban plaza itself, stairs shall have a minimum width of 10 feet.

An urban plaza or portion of an urban plaza extending through the block and connecting 2 streets which are parallel or within 45 degrees of being parallel to each other shall have a minimum width of 40 feet.

Any portion of a building wall adjoining such urban plaza for a length greater than 125 feet shall be limited to a maximum height of 85 feet above the urban plaza level, and above such height the building shall be set back not less than 15 feet from the urban plaza boundary, provided that such restriction shall not apply to any building wall adjoining an urban plaza which urban plaza has a minimum width of 75 feet.

Access for the Physically Disabled

There shall be at least 1 path of travel to each of the following:

- the major portion of the urban open space
- any building lobby accessible to the urban open space
- any use that may be present on, or adjacent to, the urban open space

Such paths shall have a minimum width of 5 feet, except where specific provisions require a greater width, free and clear of all obstructions.

Ramps are to be provided alongside any stairs or steps for such paths. Ramps shall have a minimum width of 36 inches, a slope of not greater than 1 in 12, a non-skid surface, and, for open-edged ramps, a 2-inch-high safety curb. At each end of a ramp there shall be a level area, which may be public sidewalk, at least 5 feet long.

All stairs or ramps within such paths shall provide handrails. Handrails shall be 32 inches high, have a midrail 22 inches high, and shall extend at least 18 inches beyond the stair or ramp ends.

Where stairs are used to effect changes of grade for such paths, they shall have closed risers, no projecting nosings, a maximum riser height of 7.5 inches, and a minimum tread width of 11 inches.

Food Facilities; Permitted Obstructions

Urban open space shall be unobstructed

from its lowest level to the sky except for the following obstructions, which are permitted only in urban plazas and open air concourses, but not permitted in sidewalk widenings: any features, equipment, and appurtenances normally found in public parks and playgrounds, such as fountains and reflecting pools, waterfalls, sculptures and other works of art, arbors, trellises, benches, seats, trees, planting beds, litter receptacles, drinking fountains, and bicycle racks; open air cafes; kiosks; outdoor furniture; lights and lighting stanchions; flag poles; public telephones; temporary exhibitions; awnings; canopies; bollards; and subway station entrances which may include escalators. Kiosks, open air cafes, and open air amphitheaters and ice-skating rinks which charge admission may be placed within the area of an urban open space upon certification by the Chairman of the City Planning Commission and the Board of Estimate to the Commissioner of Buildings.

Where a kiosk is provided, it shall be a 1-story structure, predominantly of light materials, such as metal, glass, plastic, or fabric which does not exceed 150 square feet in area.

Where an open air cafe is provided it shall be a permanently unenclosed eating or drinking place, permitted by applicable district regulations, which may have waiter or table service, and is open to the sky except that it may have a temporary fabric roof in conformance with the Building Code.

An open air cafe must be accessible from all sides where there is a boundary with the remainder of the urban open space.

An open air cafe may occupy an aggregate area not more than 20 percent of the total area of the urban open space.

No kitchen equipment shall be installed within an open air cafe. Kitchen equipment may be contained in a kiosk adjoining the open air cafe.

An open air cafe qualifying as a permitted obstruction shall be excluded from the definition of floor area.

Outdoor eating services or uses occupying kiosks may serve customers on urban open space through open windows.

For wheelchair users, where drinking fountains are placed in an urban open space, at least one fountain shall be 30 inches high, be hand and foot operated, and display the International Symbol of Access.

Maintenance

The building owner shall be responsible for the maintenance of the urban open space including, but not limited to, the confinement of permitted obstructions, litter control, and the care and replacement of vegetation within the zoning lot and in the street sidewalk area adjacent to the zoning lot.

Performance Bond

Prior to obtaining any certificate of occupancy from the Department of Buildings, the building owner shall provide to the Comptroller of the City of New York, a performance bond or the City securities to ensure the mandatory tree planting, movable seating and the litter-free maintenance of the urban open space including the replacement of such trees and movable furniture during the life of the development.

In the event of a failure in the required performance, the Chairman of the City Planning Commission shall notify the building owner in writing of such failure and shall stipulate the period of time in which the building owner has to correct the failure. If the failure is not corrected in the stipulated time the Chairman may declare the building owner in default in the required performance, and the City may enforce the obligation by whatever means may be appropriate to the situation, including letting contracts for doing any required planting, installation or maintenance and paying all labor, material and other costs connected with such work from the bond or City securities the building owner is required to provide.

Plaque

A plaque or other permanent sign shall be displayed in a prominent location on any urban open space for which a bonus is granted. Such sign shall indicate number of trees, and number of movable chairs, and any other features whose listing may be required by the City Planning Commission, the name of the owner and whomever he has designated to maintain the urban open space.

Existing Plazas

For plazas built prior to this amendment, kiosks and cafes may be placed within the area of the plaza upon certification by the chairman of the City Planning Commission and the Board of Estimate that such uses would promote public use and enjoyment, stabilize desirable uses in the surrounding area, are part of a general improvement including more seating and landscaping, and that the uses will be maintained by the owner.

Other Provisions

Location and orientation: Southern exposure is required wherever possible. To protect the continuity of the street wall, the frontage a plaza can occupy is restricted when there are other large spaces nearby.

Proportional restrictions: To discourage strip plazas, width of plazas must not be less than a third of the length.

Open-air concourses: These apply to spaces adjacent to subway stations and were written with the proposed Second Avenue subway in mind. They call for a sunken plaza at mezzanine level of no less than 4,000 square feet nor more than 8,000. At street level there should be walkways at least 20 feet wide, and, space permitting, a street-level plaza.

Residential Plazas (Enacted in 1977)

The intent is to create, in high density residential areas, plazas which are integrated with the street environment, and which accommodate activities and relaxation. These new provisions encourage public plazas to be accessible, inviting, sunlit, safe and beautifully landscaped.

Orientation

All developments shall provide southern exposure where possible and maximum sunlight in primary space. Other exposures are permitted only when southern exposure is not possible.

Access

All primary spaces shall be accessible directly from an adjoining public sidewalk along at least 50 percent of the total street frontage.

All primary spaces shall be accessible to the public at all times, except that for a primary space having only 1 narrow street frontage or a primary space which links 2 streets that are parallel or are within 45 degrees of being parallel, access may be restricted between the hours of 8:00 P.M. and 8:00 A.M. Such access may be restricted by the use of horizontal railings and/or vertical members and lockable gates.

Access for the physically disabled: There shall be at least 1 path of travel to major portions of primary space. All paths shall have a minimum width of 5 feet. Ramps shall be provided alongside any stairs or steps which provide access to or within primary spaces. All stairs or ramps within such paths shall provide handrails.

Where stairs are used to effect changes of grade for such paths they shall have closed risers, no projecting nosings, a maximum riser height of 7.5 inches, and a minimum tread width of 11 inches.

Elevation

All primary spaces shall be located at an elevation not more than 3 feet above or below the curb level of the nearest adjoining sidewalk.

When the size of a primary space is 8,000 square feet or more, a maximum of 25 percent of its area may be located at an elevation more than 3 feet above or below the nearest adjoining sidewalk.

Lighting

All primary spaces shall be illuminated at an overall minimum average level of not less than 2 horizontal foot candles during the hours of darkness.

Mandatory Amenities

Seating: All primary spaces shall provide a minimum of 1 linear foot of seating for each 30 square feet of the primary space. Such seating shall have a minimum depth of 1 foot 4 inches. Seating with backs at least 1 foot high shall have a minimum depth of 1 foot 2 inches. Seating 2 feet 6 inches or more in depth shall count as double, provided there is access on both sides.

For the benefit of handicapped persons, a minimum of 10 percent of the required seating shall have backs.

Seating higher than 3 feet or lower than 1 foot above the level of the adjacent walking surface shall not count towards meeting the seating requirements. Movable seating or chairs may be credited as 2

feet 6 inches of linear seating per chair. Movable seating shall not exceed 50 percent of the total required.

Steps shall not count towards the seating requirements.

The top of walls, including but not limited to those which bound planting beds, fountains or pools, may be counted as seating when they conform to the dimensional standards set forth herein.

Tree planting: All primary spaces shall provide a minimum of 1 tree per 1,000 square feet of primary space area.

Bicycle parking facilities: All primary spaces shall provide bicycle parking facilities. There shall be facilities for parking 2 bicycles for every 1,000 square feet of primary space.

Drinking fountain: All primary spaces shall provide at least 1 drinking fountain.

Additional Amenities

In addition to the mandatory amenities required above, all primary spaces shall provide at least 2 of the amenities listed in this section. These amenities are to be provided in addition to, and not in place of, those amenities required.

Tree planting: A minimum of 1 tree per 2,000 square feet of primary space area.

Planting: Planters, including hanging planters, or planting beds with seasonal flowers, shrubs, ivy, or other plants occupying a total area not less than 150 square feet for each 1,000 square feet of primary space. The area occupied by an individual planter that is permanent in nature, or a planting bed, shall be at least 30 square feet with a depth of soil of at least 2 feet.

Grass and other ground cover: A total of 150 square feet of grass or other ground cover for each 1,000 square feet of primary space.

Gametables: Game tables and seating to accomodate 16 persons for the primary space for each zoning lot.

Artwork: A work of art, such as sculpture, for the primary space for each zoning lot.

Fountains and pools: An ornamental fountain or a reflection pool occupying an area not less than 300 square feet for the primary space for each zoning lot.

Play equipment: 1 play apparatus or facility such as cross bars, climbers, swings, sandbox, paddle pool or similar play facility, for each 1,000 square feet of primary space area.

When this amenity is chosen, the mandatory trees may be reduced to half the required amount.

Open air cafe: An open air cafe, which shall be a permanently unenclosed eating or drinking place as permitted by applicable district regulations, which may have waiter or table service.

An open air cafe shall occupy not more than 20 percent of the total area of the primary space.

Kiosk: A kiosk, which shall be a 1-story structure, which including roof areas does not exceed 100 square feet in area, and be predominantly of light materials such as glass, plastic, metal or fabric.

Optional Amenities

The primary space may also include additional numbers of the amenities mentioned above and other amenities such as arbors, trellises, litter receptables, outdoor furniture, light stands, flag poles, public telephones, awnings, canopies, bollards, subway station entrances, and drinking fountains which are operable by wheelchair users.

The total area occupied by all amenities, mandatory, additional and optional, shall not exceed 60 percent of the total primary space area of the residential plaza.

Residual Space

Residual space shall abut a public sidewalk or a primary space and shall be developed either as a landscaped visual amenity or as a usable space for the general public in accordance with the provisions of this section. Not more than 40 percent of the total area of residential plaza on a zoning lot shall be developed as residual space.

Northern Plaza

A northern plaza shall provide at least 2 of the following amenities:

Planters or planting beds with seasonal flowers, shrubs, ivy, or other plants occupying an area not less than 150 square feet per 1,000 square feet of a northern plaza.

A work of art such as sculpture, for each northern plaza.

An ornamental fountain or a reflecting pool occupying an area not less than 300 square feet for each northern plaza.

A pavilion, which is a 1-story structure for the use of the public, constructed predominantly of transparent materials such as glass or plastic.

Optional Amenities: A northern plaza may also include additional numbers of the amenities mentioned above and other amenities such as arbors, trellises, litter receptacles, outdoor furniture, light stands, flag poles, public telephones, awnings, canopies, bollards, subway station entrances, and drinking fountains which are operable by wheelchair users.

Retail Continuity

When the front building wall of a development is at least 50 feet in length and fronts upon a wide street, a minimum of 50 percent of such front building wall shall be occupied by commercial uses, as permitted by district regulations.

Floor Area Bonus for a Plaza

In the district indicated, for each square foot of plaza the total floor area permitted on that zoning lot may be increased by 6 square feet.

Maintenance

Detailed requirements are similar to those for office building plazas. Builders must post performance bond to insure adequate maintenance. A plaque must be displayed giving the public full information on the amenities required.

Notes

Introduction

Two basic works of observation are Edward T. Hall's *The Hidden Dimension* (New York: Doubleday & Co., 1966) and Robert Sommer's *Personal Space: the Behavioral Basis of Design* (Englewood Cliffs, N.J.: Prentice-Hall, 1969).

Of the design professions, landscape architects have been the most interested in the study of people, and the journal *Landscape Architecture* has published some excellent articles, among them: John T. Lyle, "People Watching in Parks" (October 1970); Sidney Brower, "Streetfront and Sidewalk" (July 1973); Nancy Linday, "It All Comes Down to a Place to Sit and Watch" (November 1978). Editor Grady Clay, himself an excellent observer, has recently written *Alleys: A Hidden Resource* (Louisville: Cross Section Publishers, 1979).

The Project for Public Spaces has used direct observation and time-lapse photography for a series of excellent studies of key public spaces, ranging from Harlem's 125th Street to visitors centers at the National Parks. Reports are available on all their studies; for a list, and a brochure on their techniques, write to Project for Public Spaces, Suite 201, 875 Avenue of the Americas, New York, New York 10001.

Chapter 1: The Life of Plazas

The frequency with which people form groups of various sizes is remarkably consistent—in particular, the proportion of people in threes. Over a two year-period, studies of the distribution of people in groups showed the following:

	12 Plazas	Seagram's Plaza
In twos	67%	60%
In threes	21%	21%
In fours or more	12%	19%

These are people sitting: for people standing the proportion in large groups is smaller, but the distributions are similarly consistent, and they don't vary much according to the setting. In his Australian study, Ciolek found 71.3 percent in twos: 19 percent in threes; 9.2 percent in fours or more. This tallies closely with distributions observed in similar studies in the U.S. and Europe. William H. Whyte, assisted by Margaret Bemiss, "New York and Tokyo: A Study in Crowding," in Hidetosh Kato, ed., in collaboration with William H. Whyte and Randolph David, *A Comparative Study of Street Life.* (Tokyo: The Research Institute for Oriental Cultures, Gakushuin University, 1978). Matthew T. Ciolek, "Location of Static Gatherings in Pedestrian Areas: An Explanatory Study," Australian National University, Canberra, December 1976. Jan Gehl, "Pedestrians," ARKITEKTEN (Denmark), 1968.

Chapter 2: Sitting Space

Architect Philip Johnson:
"We designed those blocks in front of the Seagram Building so people could not sit on them, but, you see, people want to so badly that they sit there anyhow. They like that place so much that they crawl, inch along that little narrow edge of the wall. We put the water near the marble ledge because we thought they'd fall over if they sat there. They don't fall over; they get there *anyhow*."

H.K.:
"Well it's the only place you *can* sit."

P.J.:
"I know it. It never crossed Mies's mind. Mies told me afterward, 'I never dreamt people would want to sit there.'"

John W. Cook and Heinrich Klotz, *Conversations with Architects* (New York: Praeger, 1973).

Chapter 3: Sun, Trees, Wind, and Water

Improved techniques and equipment should make sun studies easier and more often used. At Ball State University in Indiana, for example, a large-scale "heliodon" has been developed to project sun angles on architectural models of one-quarter-inch scale. It can be adjusted for latitude as well as for any hour, day, month, or year.

The best work on the relationship between architecture and the natural environment is James Marston Fitch, *American Building, The Environmental Forces That Shape It*, second edition (New York: Schocken Books, 1975).

A study with a strong emphasis on the climatic aspects of urban space is Don C. Miles, with Robert S. Cook, Jr., and Cameron B. Roberts, *Plazas for People* (New York: Project for Public Spaces, 1978). Based on an analysis of Seattle spaces, the study shows the shortcomings of the standard plaza format in places where there is a good bit of rain and wind: it proposes designs sensitively tailored to these realities.

Additional research further indicates that we hear what we think we ought to hear. In connection with the new Philip Morris building going up across 42nd Street near Grand Central Station, I was asked to get decibel counts, the place being regarded as one of the very noisiest in the city. It certainly looks noisy. But the meter, surprisingly, recorded very moderate noise levels. Two years hence the place will look quite different. There will be an indoor park at the corner and the now grimy facade of Grand Central Station will be clean and white. The place will look much better, and for that reason it may sound much better. I would bet that people will perceive the area as much less noisy, whether it actually is or not.

Chapter 4: Food

One problem is that the outdoor cafe has come to be considered something of a cliché. Some years ago architectural renderings of ideal squares, plazas, and spaces almost always featured an outdoor cafe, Paris-style kiosk, a hurdy-gurdy man, and several children holding balloons. This is low fashion now. In a design competition for the redoing of the W.R. Grace plaza several years ago, some 260 proposals were submitted from architectural schools. Of these, only six included anything as rudimentary as chairs and tables, and only one of these made the finals. Several architects on the eminent jury commented favorably on the absence of such "banal" features. No proposal was adopted. What the plaza still lacks are chairs and tables for outdoor eating.

Chapter 5: The Street

I have a special reason for citing *The Exploding Metropolis* (Garden City, N.Y.: Doubleday & Co., 1958), for I edited the *Fortune* series on which it was based. I am hardly impartial, but I do think it was a bit ahead of its time, and one big reason was getting Jane Jacobs, then of *Architectural Forum,* to undertake a major piece on downtown. She came through with a slashing attack on current planning dogma, a spirited affirmation of the street that it scorned, and shortly thereafter went on to develop the themes in her classic *The Death and Life of Great American Cities* (New York: Random House, 1959).

An excellent book on the phyical street is Bernard Rudovsky's *Streets for People* (New York: Doubleday & Co., 1964). The first part is a testy put-down of the U.S. pedestrian, but the main text on the functional pleasures of Italian streets is splendid.

A good exploration of the potentials for contemporary streets is Roberto G. Brambilla's *More Streets for People* (New York: Italian Art and Landscape Foundation, 1973). With Gianni Longo, he has followed through with reports on pedestrian malls, car-free zones, and similar approaches here and abroad, published by the GPO and the Whitney Library of Design.

The pioneering study on the pedestrian as a transportation unit is John J. Fruin's *Pedestrian Planning and Design*. It is, unfortunately, out of print. But Fruin has been continuing his research, and an expanded study is in the works.

A definitive work on the imbalance between pedestrian and vehicular space, and what should be done about it, is the Regional Plan Association study by Boris S. Pushkarev and Jeffrey M. Zupan, *Urban Space for Pedestrians* (Cambridge: M.I.T. Press, 1975). Methodologically, the study is interesting for its use of aerial photography to chart pedestrian volumes. Our group, The Street Life Project, was studying several of the same areas at the time, using a combination of streets counts and time-lapse photography. Results of both studies matched closely.

Frederick Law Olmsted had a very strong appreciation for the street. He saw the streets bordering Central Park as an "outer park" and insisted they not be cut off from the park itself. When the Commissioner of Central Park instructed him to erect some sort of barrier, he answered:

It is not desirable that this outer park should be separated by any barrier more than a common stone curb from the adjoining roadways. It is still more undesirable in the interest of those who are to use it that it should be separated more than is necessary from the interior park. ... The trees which grow upon it are used in design as a part of the scenery of the main park, adding to its beauty, attractiveness and value. The scenery of the main park should much more be made to add to the beauty, attractiveness and value of the outer park. As far as it is practicable the two should be incorporated as one whole, each being part of the other.

As for the iron fences, he suggested:

I consider the iron fence to be unquestionably the ugliest that can be used. If on the score of utility, it must be used then the less the better, and certainly where used, it should not be elaborated and set up on high, and made large and striking as if it were something admirable in itself, and had better claims to be noticed than the scenery which it crosses and obscures.

Excerpt from a letter to the Board of Commissioners of Central Park, April 1860. Frederick Law Olmsted, *Forty Years of Landscape Architecture: Central Park,* edited by Frederick Law Olmsted and Theodora Kimball (Cambridge: M.I.T. Press, 1975, paperback).

Our studies show that wherever plazas have both sunken space and space at street level, the street-level space is much preferred. The J. C. Penney Building is typical: the sunken plaza accounts for 25 percent of the space, only 13 percent of the sitters. At the General Motors Building the disparity is even greater, even more so when the standees at the railings are counted.

The distribution of people at the First National Bank of Chicago plaza shows an amphitheater pattern similar to that of Rockefeller Plaza. At a time when there were approximately 800 people sitting, we found that 45 percent were in the lower plaza, 15 percent on the lower steps heading down, 40 percent on the upper steps and mezzanine level. Our findings meshed with those of a study by Professor Albert Rutledge and a group of his students of the Department of Landscape Architecture, University of Illinois, Urbana. Using a basic "pad and pencil" methodology, in a relatively short period of time they came up with a fine evaluation of how the plaza works and a set of recommendations that could make it work better. ("First National Bank Plaza: A Pilot Study in Post Construction Evaluation," June 1975.)

At the Citicorp sunken plaza and surrounding steps and ledges, the amphitheater effect is quite marked. During a summer lunch-time concert staged in the plaza, the people were distributed as follows: about 80 were on the lowest level, another 80 or so on the first set of steps, about 90 on the next level and main steps, about 150 on the ledges at street level. Total: 400 people.

Chapter 6: The "Undesirables"

New York's proposed Madison Avenue mall was beaten down in part because of undesirables. There was a two-week trial period, which our cameras recorded. They showed clearly that the people using the street were the people who worked and shopped in the area. But some retailers saw undesirables—"hippies," in particular. While I was talking to one shop owner, she noted several young people in blue jeans who were out in the street taking notes. "There they are," she said, pointing to our observers. Mayor John Lindsay invited retailers to a meeting at which I showed our film of the trial period. Some retailers still saw undesirables. One accused me of doctoring the film to eliminate evidence.

There is a reason far more compelling than fear of undesirables for the outward moves of corporations. Several years ago I made a study of top executives' place of residence prior to their corporation's move from the city. I found that the correlation between the place of residence and the new headquarters site was 90 percent. There was a particularly strong concentration of executives in a six-square-mile area bounded by three golf clubs in Fairfield County, Connecticut. Average distance from residence to new headquarters: seven miles. William H. Whyte, "End of the Exodus," *New York,* September 20, 1976.

The safety-accident records at both Paley and Greenacre Parks have been excellent. The only occurrences have been some scrapes and bruises. Neither park has ever had a claim made against it for injury or any other cause. This has had little reflection in insurance companies' liability rates, however. Greenacre carries insurance for top liability of $6 million at a premium cost of $2,200 a year. Paley carries coverage for $10 million at a cost of $2,800.

An observant account of how people self-police a place that's good to them is Amanda Burden's *Greenacre Park* (New York: Project for Public Spaces, 1978).

We have observed one beneficent use of surveillance cameras. One of the street people we've known is Harold, a troubled young man who carried a microphone and at corners staged broadcasts to the world. People jeered and laughed at him when he did. One day he saw a TV camera on a plaza. He was entranced; thereafter, from time to time, he would go and stage broadcasts to the unjeering camera.

For a perceptive study of teenage "undesirables," see Nancy Linday, "Drawing Socio-Economic Lines in Central Park: An Analysis of New York's Cultural Clashes," *Landscape Architecture,* November 1977. Back in 1973, we were asked by then Parks Commissioner Richard Clurman to undertake a study of the troubles at Bethesda Fountain. It had become the central rendezvous for Hispanic teenagers

and there were problems with dope and vandalism. One of our best observers, Nancy Linday, spent the summer there. She found that most of the time the teenagers were making a good use of the fountain area, however raucous they might seem to the tourists who came to gawk at them. Among her recommendations: work *with* the teen-agers; involve them in maintenance projects; have more "mayors."

Some Supreme Court cases on public rights in private places, namely, shopping centers, are: (1) *Amalgamated Food Employees Union Local 590 et. al.* v. *Logan Valley Plaza, Inc. et. al.,* 391 vs. 308 (1977); (2) *Marsh* v. *Alabama,* 326 vs. 501 (1946); (3) *Lloyd Corp. Ltd.* v. *Tanner et. al.,* 407 vs. 551 (1971). I am indebted to Mark Shuster of the Massachusetts Institute of Technology for his monograph on these decisions. As a useful summary of the legal points involved, he cites the *Harvard Law Review*'s article on the Supreme Court 1971 Term (*HLR* 86: 122 N 1972). It emphasizes the changing socioeconomics, noting: "Expression of a general political or social nature, though it may well be unrelated to any use or purpose of the property sought as a forum, nonetheless needs as much protection from threatened displacement of traditional first amendment forums caused by socioeconomic developments as does speech related to the functions of property."

Chapter 7: Effective Capacity

See City of New York, Department of City Planning, Urban Design Group, *New Life for Plazas* (April 1975), the complete text, illustrated, of the zoning provisions adopted in 1975 for office-building spaces; *Plazas for People* (May 1977), the illustrated text of the provisions adopted in 1977 for residential construction.

Cities that are contemplating incentives

for small parks would do well to make requirements a bit more flexible than we did. With the benefit of hindsight, it is now apparent that the specifications were a bit too stiff—in particular, the requirements that small parks be accessible at all times. Paley and Greenacre are not. Both have gates that are closed at night. Managements that provide comparable amenities should be able to do the same, or, alternatively, to store away the movable chairs and tables at closing time. Such a course has been approved by New York City for the plaza and outdoor cafe of the office building at 1166 Avenue of the Americas.

Chapter 8: Indoor Spaces

For a minority report on indoor spaces, see Suzanne Stephens, "The Market at Citicorp, New York City," *Progressive Architecture,* December 1978.

Chapter 9: Concourses and Megastructures

In a trenchant critique of megastructures, William G. Conway, a former associate of architect John Portman, noted the effect they have on the spaces between them. In "The Case Against Urban Dinosaurs" (*Saturday Review,* May 14, 1977), he holds that these visions of a controlled environment reveal the designer's hostility to the cities he professes to save. In Atlanta, he writes, "the five huge architectural jewels in the South's queen city are transforming her crown into fool's gold. This reverse alchemy is laying waste the downtown *between* the megastructures. In so doing it obeys the laws of economics now ignored by the project sponsors and by the city officials who clamor for more megastructures without first knowing the effects of those already constructed."

For a discussion of the street as a market,

see Barbara Petrocci (York University, Toronto), "The New Urban Marketplace: Street Fairs and Farmers' Markets Revisited," a paper presented at the annual meeting of the American Sociological Association, September 1978.

Chapter 10: Smaller Cities and Places

An excellent evaluation of urban spaces across the country has been provided by August Heckscher, with Phyllis Robinson, *Open Spaces: the Life of American Cities* (New York: Harper & Row, 1977). A former New York City park commissioner, Mr. Heckscher has an especially keen eye for the troubles and pleasures of center-city parks.

A fine critical analysis of downtown development, and zoning's role in it, is planner Kenneth Halpern's *Downtown USA: Urban Design in Nine American Cities* (New York: Whitney Library of Design, 1978).

In a forthcoming book, lawyer Robert S. Cook, Jr., will look at downtown development; the effects, good and otherwise, of incentive zoning and design controls; the lessons to be heeded.

Chapter 11: Triangulation

I am indebted to Hans-Bernd Zimmerman for his perceptive study of the social patterns of Brooklyn's Esplanade, done as part of the doctoral program in environmental psychology at the Graduate Center of The City University of New York.

for Jan 25 w.3
    6~75   94-101